TWICE IN LOVE

REVIEWS

The book is surprising in its openness and honesty, and succeeds in portraying the sentiments and difficulties of young Tel Avivians searching for their personal salvation.

–David Zoldan,
Haaretz newspaper, Jan. 2017

This is the best book explaining Judaism published in recent years, especially on the issues of modesty and the status of women in Judaism.

–Rabbi Shlomo Raanan,
Chairman of the Ayelet HaShachar organization

I believe that you have been truly blessed with the gift of writing so that people can understand, at eye level, matters that are so necessary for many of our Jewish brethren.

–Yonadav Kaploun, poet

This is a very important book for you to publish, exactly as written, and takes priority over your work of [Talmudic] insights. Every work is important, but we have many rabbis and yeshiva heads today who publish their Talmudic novellae - whilst this type of work is unique and very lacking.

–The Jerusalem Gaon Rabbi Shlomo Fischer *zt"l*,
Dean of Yeshivat Itri

Twice in Love
by Meir Dorfman
Translated by Rabbi Hillel Fendel

Copyright © 2022 by Meir Dorfman

Book design by Riki Greiniman
Cover design by the Virtual Paintbrush
Edited by Nechama and Dr. Paul Gluck
Translation consulting by Dr. Morris Dorfman and
Rabbi Nechemia Klein

Published by Ktav Publishing House and Targum Press
Distributed by Ktav Publishing House

ISBN 978-1-60280-480-7

The author can be contacted at
meirdorfman@gmail.com

Printed in Israel.
⊘CONTROLᴾ
+97229971070

TWICE IN LOVE

*"How come twice when I have lost my love
altogether, and why is a secular individual forbidden
to do what is permissible to a religious person?"*

A collection of e-mail exchanges with
younger Tel Aviv residents on the search for their
direction in life and piercing questions
regarding Judaism and faith

MEIR DORFMAN

Translated By Hillel Fendel

CONTENTS

PREFACE

"I LIGHT CANDLES BUT I DRIVE..."

I heard three similar stories within a week. The first story was told to me by a very talented young woman, born and raised in Israel, who embarked on a journey around the world. During her travels she met a very nice young man - educated like her and a true gentleman. She was planning to return that week to his country, move in with him, and look for work there. She mentioned in passing that he is not Jewish; it wasn't something that disturbed her. Her 96-year-old grandfather took this very badly, she said, but she doesn't understand why. Perhaps it has to do with age, she figures, or the thinking of the older generation…

She grew up in a very Zionistic home, she said, but on a personal level she feels that life with this boyfriend is right for her, and her children will then be part of the greater outside world. "The main thing is the person," she said. "It's not as if I am so Jewish anyway…," she concluded, pointing to her not overly modest clothing.

She told me this following my weekly lecture on insights into the weekly Torah portion and their relevance to our own lives. The lecture takes place in "HaMakom (The Place) – the Center for Culture and Spirit" located in Tel Aviv, frequented by a variety of artists, journalists, economists, scientists, lawyers and many other young Tel Avivians.

The second story was told to me by a member of my army reserves unit when we met at an emergency call-up during Operation Tzuk Eitan (Protective Edge). He had been traveling in South America where he met a very nice young woman at one of the clubs. They are now living together in Israel, planning to get married outside of Israel and settle there. She is not Jewish. He plans to remain a Zionist and possibly even return to Israel whenever he's called for reserves duty. His mother noted that her grandchildren will not be Jewish, but she will respect his decisions.

The third story was told to me by one of the younger members of the same unit. Same thing; it happened during his travels following his army service. He defined his outlook: "I actually like tradition, but not religion."

Every so often I perform as a Cantor or singer in Jewish communities in the Diaspora, primarily in remote, out-of-the-way places. I often sit informally with the audience during the long nights that follow these events for some heart-to-heart talks, and there I hear many such stories. But hearing them now, back here in Israel, and with much greater frequency than before - that's something very new for me. I think to myself: "It's a fact: Drastic changes are happening here." And by the way, the changes are happening in all directions, including a tremendous, growing interest in Torah study – even within the non-religious sector. You can see this all over the country, and especially in HaMakov in Tel Aviv.

Every week, I take a bus to HaMakom from Jerusalem to Tel Aviv. Sometimes I feel that this bus route, more than it connects between cities, actually connects between vastly differing cultures and sectors of the Jewish population that are so different that one does not understand the other's language.

This book focuses on the boundaries between these sectors, on seeking a path and looking for answers. I was once waiting on line for a bus, and standing near me were two women engaged in conversation. Suddenly a religious-looking man cut in front and made his way to the front of the line. One of the women immediately shouted out to him, "Shame on you! And you're even religious - with a kippah (yarmulke)!" The second one responded: "Are you really surprised? They wear the kippah just for show." I identified with these "secular" women's perception of Jewish Law, according to which it demands higher ethical standards.

This book is not written as an ordinary book, but is rather a collection of email correspondence between me and students who attend my lectures. Out of thousands of emails, I picked questions that came up most frequently. Of course, all personal details and identifying information have been altered, and permission to publish was granted for each exchange.

I do not claim to have all the answers. I rather spend time listening to questions that we all have, so that we may experience the search together and try to "translate" the Torah and Jewish Law into present-day language.

Ignorance is a primary source of many contradictions that people find between Torah and life. But this is not their only explanation; we are also missing the Jewish experience today. Judaism has always been transmitted from generation to generation through warm, personal connection. This warm intimacy has almost disappeared. The information remains, and it is vast, and available - but this is only a small part of Judaism.

When I used to approach my Rabbis with questions, they would often not immediately respond with answers. Instead, they said, "Let's go and study this topic together; let's open books, tell me your opinion, and we'll clarify it together." I am speaking even of heads of large Yeshivot and those who render rulings for thousands. They find the time and have the desire to study with a young student. This is the extraordinary way that love of Torah is passed down.

With this in mind, I have not shortened the lengthy questions, and I have not softened their pointedness, for the distress apparent in the question is no less important than the answer. We are journeying together. I hope I can succeed in transmitting this not so well-known method via this book.

Is this book intended for religious or for non-religious readers? I believe that in today's generation, the deep questions that trouble all of us are identical; the difference is only that they are expressed more sharply in the "secular" population. Every human being deals with questions of how to contend with loneliness, with the search for an intimate relationship that comes from the highest soul levels, with reservations and uncertainties regarding belief, the existence of a higher-level entity, personal providence, grasping onto eternity, and the enduring of the soul. We all wonder: How can I discover my unique task in this world? What is my goal? How do I make the most of myself and my talents? What about work versus leisure, family, children, the meaning of Jewish identity in the global world, sadness and joy, improving my character, dealing with various sorts of crises, death or illness of a close relative or friend, G-d forbid, and so much more.

We expect that the ancient wisdom of Judaism will provide a strong and relevant statement that addresses these issues. Furthermore, I believe that every Jew, whoever and wherever he may be, wants to be able to identify with his Judaism, to view his Jewishness as beautiful, ethical, and of superior wisdom, and to find in it a meaningful life based on strong values and a tradition passed down in the most honorable manner. If this book will help make some order out of this confusion and strengthen even a small part of our Jewish identity – this will be sufficient.

Countless books have been written that focus on explaining the various disciplines in Judaism.

Nevertheless, I often encounter difficulties when I want to recommend an appropriate book for my students. Most of the books in this field are written in the old style of the Beit Midrash: they are filled with sources, mainly focus inward, and are primarily understood by those on the inside – in terms of both content and language – where the answer takes precedence over the question. I hope that authentic correspondence and open and piercing letters from my students will not miss the mark. Due to the great variety of questioners, the writing style is not consistent, and I therefore recommend considering the option of skipping around among the chapters.

It is my hope that teachers, educators, Rabbis, and philosophers will be able to feel the heartbeat of the "questions of the generation" through this book. I can honestly say that the questions collected here represent an accurate sampling of the hundreds of questions I have received.

I have been privileged, throughout my life, to learn Torah and Judaism from the entire spectrum of Torah teachers. I believe that the novelty in this book lies in its being a new "translation" of that same old Judaism - tradition passed down through the generations translated into the language of today's values. As strange as this may sound, approval for this book was given by the greatest Jewish philosophers and *poskim* (issuers of Halakhic rulings) from all parts of the spectrum. This is what I refer to as "mainstream Judaism."

Many thanks to the Torah giants Rabbi Shlomo Fischer and Rabbi Zalman Nehemiah Goldberg for their advice and encouragement in the publishing of this book. Thanks to the poet Yonadav Kaploun, to the head of Ulpanat Bnei Akiva in Pisgat Ze'ev Rabbi Refael Kuperstoech, and to Nili Trabelsi for their share in this endeavor. Thanks to Dr. Hagi Ben-Artzi for his encouragement and counsel, and to the entire publishing staff of Steimatzky for their thoroughness and professionalism.

Although this book was written on my own accord, I would like to thank the staff of HaMakom as well as its administration, the thousands of people who pass through its gates, and the hundreds of students who remained in touch with me and raised pointed questions.

Thanks to my children for their cooperation throughout the entire process. And great thanks of course to my loyal partner over the past 25 years, who has stood by and with me in all my endeavors, and most recently through all the difficulties that naturally arose between the dream and its realization – my wife Yael.

Meir Dorfman

INTRODUCTION TO THE ENGLISH EDITION

I performed in an inspirational concert one night in one of the Jewish communities in Texas, and afterwards I traveled back with a man who had been in the audience. It was quite late at night, the day before Yom Kippur, and he cried the whole way. I inquired as to the reason, and he said, "Everything just opened up inside me..." I said I was sorry if I had brought that about, but he said, "No, it's good that it's all out in the open for me now. I really believe that this pain marks the start of my recovery and my way out, and that the difficult questions now facing me will bring me to a new, better phase in my life."

This poignantly reminded me of the words of the Kotzker Rebbe. On the verse, "He who increases knowledge, increases pain" (Eccl. 1,18), the Kotzker said: 'So what if pain is increased? It's well worth it to increase knowledge, even if it also adds pain.'

The correspondences in this book took place between myself and residents of Tel Aviv, who shared with me their deepest and most personal questions and uncertainties. In the few years since Steimatzky published the book in Hebrew, many thousands of copies have been sold, in all sectors of the populace. During this period I learned that the topics covered in the book are actually quite universal. It turns out that everyone in this generation asks the same questions, faces and deals with similar difficulties, and experiences the same longings. When I was asked by several congregational rabbis and high school teachers abroad to have some of the chapters translated, I realized there was a need to translate the work and disseminate it in the world.

The first to raise the idea of translation was the Rabbanit Miriam Feldman, principal of a girls' high school in Atlanta and the wife of the rabbi there. How I arrived in Atlanta in the first place was a matter of Divine providence: I had actually been in Savannah for a concert when a strong hurricane hit the city - resulting in my temporary "evacuation," together with many others, to the Jewish community in Atlanta. There I was privileged both to perform for Rabbi Ilan Feldman's congregation, and to greatly enjoy the Feldmans' wonderful and gracious home hospitality. I was also happy to have some long and very illuminating talks with Rabbi Ilan, a "man of spirit," and with his son-in-law Rabbi Yitzchak Tendler. And so it was that the idea of translating the book began to roll around in my mind via a hurricane that G-d rolled about in a place so far from my home. It continued to take shape in talks with the members of the Savannah Kollel Torah study group, especially Rabbi Avi Nitekman, all of whose good counsel was most helpful. And its final seal of approval came as the result of my talks with overseas students studying at Hebrew University in Jerusalem, who sought answers to the very same questions discussed in the book.

Many Torah scholars and leaders advised,

encouraged and assisted in the process, including: Rabbi Doron Peretz, Executive Chairman of the Mizrachi World Movement; Rabbi Shlomo Raanan, founder and chairman of Ayelet Hashachar; Dr. Hagi Ben-Artzi, of Bar Ilan University; Rabbi Moshe Shilat, founder of Chabad on Campus - Israel; R. Tzvi (Enrique) and Dr. Annette-Hanna Medresh of Mexico; Rabbi Nachum Neriah, President of Torah Mitzion; Rabbi Avi Berman, Executive Director of OU Israel; Rabbi Shalom Mendel Shagalov of Miami; Rabbi Mark Fishman of Congregation Beth Tikvah in Montreal; and many more fine people. My thanks are hereby extended to all of them.

Further Thanks

To Rabbi Hillel Fendel, for the translation he accomplished with great skill, creativity, and a deep understanding of the content and the readership. I enjoyed the process of working with him, including our arguments and give-and-take on each chapter; at least something positive resulted from the Covid-19 closures...

To my mother-in-law Nechama Gluck, who reviewed and edited the book and its translation, and helped with wise comments and suggestions, with great dedication. I believe that her many years of work with youth as an educational psychologist left their imprint on both the content and the translation.

To translator Rabbi Nechemia Klein for his help and constructive comments.

To my father and teacher Dr. Moshe Dorfman for advice and solutions on critical points and literary matters – a hidden talent of his that I discovered only recently, while working on this book.

To Akiva Atwood, owner of Targum Press, and Moshe Heller, owner of Ktav Publishing House, for publishing the book with great forbearance, and for the work in distributing and marketing it. To Shira for her dedicated work.

To graphic designers Riki Greiniman for her page layout work, and Shanie Cooper for designing the cover with creativity and patience.

To all the staff members at HaMakom, The Center for Culture and Spirit, in Tel Aviv, for providing me my teaching home ever since its founding. HaMakom's activity has expanded amazingly of late, and I am privileged to engage in thousands of correspondences with my students – some of which will perhaps serve as the basis for future books.

And last but far from least, to my wife Yael – for her many precise suggestions regarding the translation, the editing, and the entire process, all of which is just a small iota of her partnership in, and support for, all my various projects.

Meir Dorfman
Jerusalem
Adar 2, 5782 / March 2022

CHAPTER 1

BITTER LONELINESS, SWEET SOLITUDE

September 23, 2012 10:42 PM

Hi Meir,

Your most recent lecture was very difficult for me. You spoke of solitude, of people who were alone in the world, beginning with Moses and the Prophet Elijah in the cave. Then you made your way to more modern personalities, such as the contemporary poet Rachel who wrote in solitude, alone in her yearnings, and rabbis who continued to write and create under all types of difficult circumstances (you mentioned someone who authored a book on the Talmud while in Siberia in which he quoted entire sections from memory). Hearing all this, I began to feel that my solitude is not at all this type of solitude. They experienced a solitude that was shining, beautiful, holy, and full. If only my solitude was so elevating and spiritual! For me, solitude is an endless sea of pain, my greatest fear, the actualization of a nightmare, the hell of day-to-day life.

Let me remove my mask: You will be surprised to discover that my fame and fortune has not eased my loneliness even one iota. The truth is that I know nothing else. I was born into loneliness.

Even during the wild and crazy days of my youth, I was truly alone. I matured into loneliness, and as the days passed, I built an external façade around myself. When my parents divorced, G-d became my best friend. However, as time went on He answered me less and less about my loneliness. I leaned on Him many times, because I was unable to lean on myself. It was all an illusion.

In the past I always feared that people would discover just how lonely I really am ... Today, I can look this fear in the face, and shout out loud: So what! Let them see, it doesn't bother me if the truth is exposed. If they wish to judge, that's their problem!

Working in the theater too is one big façade, so that no one will see what's happening inside, that everything is broken, that I have nothing to connect to. In the theater world, for some reason, they see me as a woman with depth and spirituality ... and people on the outside are convinced that acting is fulfilling, as art is for the soul, and that actors are never lonely because they are mostly surrounded by very talented people. Not quite... I also escaped to my books. I assume that because I act so well, I've convinced everyone that I live a high and noble lifestyle.

You once wrote me some examples of universal spiritual experiences that are expressed in very different ways. I then began to think that if loneliness is also a universal experience, then I would have already come to terms with it. But the passing of each day is very painful – another week, another Shabbat, and my yearning continues for someone who can save me from myself. This is not the lyrical solitude or the sweet pain that is spoken of...

I finally managed to detach myself from G-d, the One Who left me in such a sad world ... and as of now I am still alone. Most of my relationships with men have been far from healthy. Actually, not one of the men I chose for myself even saw me at all. Perhaps having a relationship is also not a refuge; maybe men want different things from a relationship than women do.

Forgive my lengthy description; loneliness constantly hovers over me like a black halo. Sometimes all I want is just to eat my Friday night meal with someone with whom I have a common language ... and some I need to sell myself cheap in exchange for a momentary hug, for a feeling of being together ... and to once again forget who I am. The supposed adoration people have for me goes right past me; it doesn't touch me, I swear. It has no meaning. The strangest thing of all is that there are people who are actually jealous of me; if only they knew just a little more...

I try to drive away all negative thoughts – every fear or idea that might weaken me my search for a perfect soul-mate. Perhaps I'm naïve, but I still dream of finding a wonderful man who suits me perfectly, and of having children (whom I'll be able to take to the theater to watch their mother on stage) – very basic dreams.

I hope I haven't upset you, but I felt that I could open up to you without having to falsely beautify the reality.

I don't know how you resolve or line up the spiritual solitude of those creative individuals, with the pain of loneliness that ordinary people such as me experience. Did these people also feel so negative? Is the lonely suffering I describe reflected at all in the sources? I'm sorry, but your beautiful lecture did not provide me with any answers to my loneliness.

See you soon,

Naama

September 24, 2012 1:14 AM

Hello Naama – and Shanah Tovah![1]

Truly a stormy and passionate letter; it touched my heart, and brought me pain and joy at the same time, because it has a positive message. If only I could help you search for the right man - though I believe that that's not the main point.

---

[1] That is, best wishes for a good, happy and meaningful new year.

Many years ago I had a conversation with the late Rabbi Shagar[2], and among other things we discussed solitude. I do not know whether you have heard of him - he was a philosopher, a Torah scholar, a Rosh Yeshiva, surrounded by students searching for direction like him. When we concluded our conversation, we left his house, and on our way to the synagogue to pray he seemed very preoccupied, perhaps engrossed in what we had discussed. He then made a very strong statement, which I assumed he hewed from the depth of his personal experience: "There are people upon whom it has been decreed to live their entire lives in solitude." What solitude could someone like him have experienced? You will certainly understand.

Let me address your question:

1. About People in Constant Search - Perhaps This is Not Even Solitude?

I can safely assume that the world I live in is very different from yours – and yet, this search, the lack of tranquility, the burning, the unwillingness to suffice with too little of that which is truly important, is something I understand and am familiar with; so it seems to me. I view this situation as something fundamental, not mere happenstance. You may not like me saying this, but I believe that you will achieve

---

[2] Known by this acronym for his name, Rabbi Shimon Gershon Rosenberg was a Torah scholar, original thinker, and founder and head of Yeshivat Siach Yitzchak in Efrat.

tranquility and calm in your life, you will find your place and the right man – but the constant burning and search will still not ease. The question will be how to use this challenge to produce sweet fruits, how to channel it to creativity rather than to sinking. When you achieve that, your difficult challenge will be transformed into a tremendous plus.

Did you ever think that perhaps this is not a matter of loneliness, but rather of meaning in life, the value of what you are involved in? Perhaps it has nothing to do with other people?

I realize that for me to judge your pain while looking on from the outside is problematic. You mentioned the poet Rachel; perhaps this is similar to one of her poems where she writes something like, "My screams became poetry for you." She was crying out in pain, and her readers were enjoying her poetry! But with all the strangeness and injustice, this was how her poems were formed; her creativity stemmed from her cries. And why did this speak to people? Because the artist's soul expresses the feelings that exists on some level within every person, as you wrote, with the only difference being that the artist is capable of expressing it with greater intensity.

The question is not whether or not you will remain alone, for it is impossible to live completely alone; rather, you must change your definitions – try to narrow down what it is that will truly give you the feeling of not being alone. Most basically, for example, you once believed that a hug would rescue you from loneliness – but what value is there in a hug from someone who does not truly love you?

I was filled with optimism from the expressions you chose, from the definitions you used - because a "soul-mate" is precisely whom you must search for, someone lonely like yourself. This appears strange – what can be the sum of a lonely man and a lonely woman? And if you compromise and settle for someone spiritually weaker than yourself, with a zest for life and creativity that is less than yours, you will continue to feel lonely.

[In Yeshivot, the majority of study time is spent in pairs, referred to as "*chavruta.*" When I was younger, I spent most of my time studying alone, without a *chavruta*. My cousin, who was studying in the same Yeshiva, also preferred studying alone. My father once jokingly said to me, "If he likes to study alone and you also prefer to study alone, perhaps you are suited for one another, so why not join together as a *chavruta*?]

2. The Difference Between Social Loneliness and Spiritual Solitude.

By the way, the Rabbi in Siberia whom I spoke about was known as the "Tzebiner Rav." I specifically mentioned him because just last week I met an elderly gentleman who had been with him in Siberia. This happened some 70 years ago, and now, many years later, this man felt the need to participate in publishing those writings. This elderly man described the suffering of that creative individual – without students, without colleagues, without books, beyond the suffering that the others in Siberia endured. The more he suffered, the greater was his heroism in dedicating himself entirely to Torah during those difficult days. This was more of a spiritual solitude than social loneliness. In your letter you slightly mix the two together, but although they are different they also affect one another.

Are you familiar with Leah Goldberg's poems on the subject? A lonely woman who is suffering her entire life writing so strongly about love; a woman without children writing the most insightful stories about the soul of the child. I recently read the book "To Leah" by Professor Amia Lieblich, a diary of a psychological journey into the persona of Goldberg. Throughout the book, her extreme spiritual solitude is apparent, on the background of her many social opportunities and the great public recognition she merited. In my opinion, in this solitude was a yearning for deep faith.

The solitude of the people I spoke about in the lecture was presumably a different experience for each of them. The cry of King David forced to flee and hide in the caves, far away from his natural surroundings, differs greatly from Elijah being pursued by Jezebel and her soldiers, perplexed by the hypocrisy of those "wavering between two views."[3] Let us compare the two: David cries from the cave, "Look to the right and see that I have no friend... no one seeks to save my life. I have cried out to You, G-d, I have said: 'You are my refuge, my portion in the land of the living'" (Psalms 142:5) – seemingly directly related to his difficult social solitude. On the other hand, Elijah's call from the cave - "They have razed Your altars and have killed Your prophets by the sword, so that I alone have remained, and they now seek to take my life" (Kings I 19:10) – is more like an expression of deep spiritual solitude.

Of course, we are imagining these situations on our level, while in truth we have no concept of the essence of their feelings and cries. But I am not convinced that their solitude was "shining and beautiful," as you wrote. The results, on the other hand, are most certainly shining and beautiful, as we see in the Book of Psalms – anyone experiencing pain is convinced that it was authored with him in mind: "My G-d, my G-d, why have You forsaken Me... I call out by day, but You answer not, and by night, but there is no respite for me..." (Psalms 22:2-3). This is a very deep cry, which has undergone fine-tuning: "Yes, things are difficult and terrible for me, but what do I make of this? I am alone – tell me for what purpose I was "granted" such aloneness? What good, despite all, can I produce from it?"

---

[3] The full story appears in Kings I 18.

3. About Belief, Aloneness, and What Lies Between Them

It's good that you left G-d if he makes your life so miserable, and for sure as time goes on you'll replace him with another One, a better G-d, one Who is loving, merciful, and maybe even sad because everyone has left Him and He is alone, and yet He doesn't despair of people...

It's not nice of me to be so cynical, but the truth is that like anything else in our lives, our faith is constantly growing and undergoing change. It is permitted and even desirable to exchange our childish and immature faith with belief that has matured with age. The simple and innocent belief that sufficed for the difficult days of your youth is no longer satisfying. Your image of G-d has not sufficiently grown up with you. Whether He is "good for you" or He is "bad for you," there is no substitute for faith; one cannot live in this world without faith. The only question is in what to have faith.

Faith is a connection, a relationship, and love, more than mere philosophy. It allows you to clarify, speak, bring up any difficulty and challenge, ask Him for answers, and listen to the voice of G-d speaking to you. You may ask yourself what He expects from you, and what you expect from Him. On a certain level it can be compared to a relationship between a couple, or to any other relationship – not in essence, but in structure.

4. Solitude as an Inner Calling to Meaning in Life

Who are these people with whom you are constantly debating about what they will or will not think, and that you don't care about them, and that you have to show them that you're strong? Why do they take up so much space in your life? How do you have so much room for them in your life when you are so lonely? You clearly still have very significant interaction with society - but note what it is like: You are in a constant state of battle - angry, explosive, leaving, hiding, removing masks. Perhaps you should find a way of life that is not a constant battle? Maybe it's good that you are "separating" from them, in favor of a true and deep meeting with your true self – Naama. Perhaps this is the first step towards true redemption from solitude. The Biblical command to "love your fellow as yourself" means first and foremost to love yourself, to accept yourself, to feel good in your own company.

In other words, it's impossible to explain your loneliness as something that simply happened, that you just "happened" not to have yet met the right person. I assume that with all you have to offer, there are many young men who would be interested in you – but they do not meet the deep needs that you described. Do you really believe that there are no men in the world who could? Clearly the problem is not that you have not yet met him, but rather that your search is connected to the wider search for self-definition, for vocation, for your place in this world from a spiritual perspective - a search that relates to your soul as well.

I believe that if you were to meet a man as lonely as yourself, you would find it easier to search for a path together with him. I am convinced that this is not a classic story of one who has not yet found the man of her dreams. Perhaps we need a different word, one that more accurately pertains to each part of your search – for the words "solitude" and "loneliness" are used by many, but they are not always referring to the same thing.

Regarding universal solitude, I recommend reading "Lonely Man of Faith" by Rabbi Dr. Yosef Dov Soloveitchik. It is inspired by the short-lived solitude of the first man in the world, as related in Genesis. He claims that loneliness is for the most part a modern western malady.

Gmar Chatima Tova,[4]

Meir

P.S. While we're on the subject, let me cite from Leah Goldberg's personal diary. Unlike you, she believed that her loneliness was a part of her. I'm just copying it here with no connection to all of the above, simply because you will understand the poem, and it also

---

[4] Between Rosh HaShanah (the first day of the year) and Yom Kippur (the Day of Atonement), these words, meaning, "May (your judgment) be sealed for the good," are a common greeting. On Rosh HaShanah mankind is judged for the coming year, and on Yom Kippur the judgment is sealed. During the days in between, one has a chance to alter a negative decree with proper repentance.

contains some beautiful expressions she uses when speaking to herself:
"You are a not-pretty woman, twenty-two years old,
An extinguished candle on the Sabbath table...
At times he knocks on the door at night,
And in the morning – you see his footprints, imprinted in the earth of a dream...
You kiss them with wounded lips,
And you do not pray that he will return again."
Wishing you Sabbath tranquility,
    Meir

Hi Meir,

    Thank you very much for answering.

    Your email shed some new light and color on solitude and loneliness, and gave it a shade of beauty and depth. This helps me on days that I feel strong, but there are days, particularly nights, when this beauty does not stand the test of pain.

    ... Regarding what you wrote about men - you are absolutely right; there are, in fact, many who want to be with me, but not one of them awakens in me the desire to want to be with them. At times I meet someone really different, a lone wolf, someone interesting and a bit wild, but with time I realize that such a person will never truly love me.

    The search drives me crazy, and gives me no

rest ... I understand that you're recommending a change in my approach and in the way I relate to the world in general. I should be more loving, relaxed, accepting. I should accept pain as well, I shouldn't be in constant opposition, I should cooperate. Perhaps you are right. It's easy for me to tell myself these things, but to actually put them into practice – that would require a complete upheaval within me, because I am a perfectionist. Perhaps I am even in love with this situation, as strange as it may sound, and I know that I must separate myself from this love.

You mentioned the Book of Psalms - this is truly something new for me. I mean I've heard of the book, but I thought it was just what the old man standing guard at the post office reads, or what religious people use in the synagogue. You aroused my curiosity, so I bought a Psalms with very nice explanations at the bottom. For example, there are many chapters expressing the desire to see the downfall of one's enemies. My first thought was, what does this have to do with me? However in the commentary and explanations I found that these are actually prayers about all the thoughts that bring us down, feelings of depression that are our worst enemy. I was able to really connect to that.

I would like to ask you about Leah's poem.

Why doesn't she want him to return?
–Naama

October 9, 2012 10:40 PM

Hi Naama,

1. Try to change the question from "Whom do I love?" to "Am I in a state of love?"

I think what you need is a "man of love." And perhaps, then, you must be "a woman of love." What I mean is that love is a state of the soul, like a radio wave that a person is tuned in to. When you are in a state of love - in "love" - you have a wide and open space for all, a world of optimism, of faith in goodness, of trust that everything is headed to a better state. It is faith in your own goodness, and faith in the goodness of others. This is something very much not abstract, and it has no room for despair.

Viewing love as "turning inward" is very inaccurate, in my opinion. The object of love is far less important than the state of love - just like the busiest people are the ones who find time for everything, while the ones who do the least never have time for anything. In other words, you're searching for a love that is a way of life, and not necessarily love for a specific person. Finding your "soul-mate" is the ultimate goal, but there are also a thousand other loves along the way. Or perhaps we can say that there exists one love with many facets branching out. I imagine you're saying to yourself, "When I find him, I'll have more room for the entire world, my life will be tranquil, happy, and optimistic." But this is your mistake, I believe – because you are not looking for "him", you're looking for a better way of life, one that is creative, rich, with much room to express the depths of your emotions, a life with lofty ideals, and the belief that you have a role in making this world a better place.

Now, try to imagine: You meet a man who is optimistic, alive, full of love for the world and for life (which does not have to be superficial and naïve), full of happiness. So first and foremost, he has room; he is a man who loves. From here to the point where he will love you is a short distance, for his heart is wide. If he is attracted to you, it means there is a strong basis for deep closeness.

If my memory serves me right, a similar idea is expressed in one of Zelda's poems: "Smitten with longings, I sought closeness of soul with no vested interests."

Perhaps I have not written anything you did not already know. It's all connected to your constant battles that I wrote about above. My heart wrenches as I think of this hardship in your life; loneliness is, in my eyes, the most difficult form of non-physical suffering. (I remember when I was single, I believed that even after I would find the woman I was searching for, I would remain sensitive to those who are lonely and would not close myself up in the ivory tower of "I have rescued myself." I'm not sure if I sufficiently kept my commitment...)

2. Why did Leah pray that he would not return?

I knew you would ask that! What's your opinion? Perhaps, since it was only a dream, the pain of waking up is not worth the few imaginary pleasant moments? Or perhaps this is an optimistic prayer that he will not return only in a dream, but in reality. I believe only a woman can truly understand such emotional depth that a woman has; you certainly will know how to interpret this better than me. I also believe it has something to do with her double life, to some extent, with the show she puts on, as you know so well how to describe. She was also a professor of stature at Hebrew University, lecturing regularly before hundreds of students. By the way, I cannot begin to imagine a show-life for so many years on end; I don't know how you're able to live like this for so long, unless you have an iron will to hide G-d knows what and from whom. It has been too long to be just a show.

Yesterday [the day after Sukkot], we prayed at the Gra Synagogue in Tel Aviv. There is an elderly rabbi there with about 103 years of life experience. When we parted he said to me: "What substance remains from all of these holidays? What of all our beautiful prayers of the festivals will we continue to recite? Only *Mashiv Haruach Umorid Hagashem* [He Who makes the wind blow and makes the rain descend[5]]. So let us dance and sing these words!" He got up and began to dance with all his might, uplifting and encouraging the young and tired congregation to join him in dancing …

So, may the rains we pray for wash away the tears, bring growth, cleanse, and purify.

Praying for your success,

Meir

---

[5] Recited daily during the winter months

CHAPTER 2

THE RELATIONSHIP BETWEEN MEN AND WOMEN IN THE TALMUD

SEPARATION? EXCLUSION? DISCRIMINATION? EMPOWERMENT?[6]

Question: "...I feel that women are second class when it comes to the synagogue, we do not take part in the prayer ceremony, and we are not given any leading roles. Our place is in the balcony or on the side, as if we had purchased a cheaper ticket".

As a rule, anyone who claims that the Talmud views men and women identically is clearly mistaken and is attempting to tailor the Talmud to populist demands. Just as anyone who claims the existence of such perfect equality in life, even as a possibility – is clearly mistaken. A male womb has not yet been created, nor have we yet met a man able to nurse a baby - and we have not even touched upon the spiritual/psychological differences between males and females.

If so, why are many under the impression that the Talmud and Jewish sources discriminate against

---

[6] For convenience, I have divided the letter into subcategories.

women? I believe that, on the face of it, the opposite is the case. When we attempt to analyze the Talmud using modern concepts, confusion results. Life may have been structured differently then, but halakhah[7] applies for all generations. Our task is to properly extract and apply the basic principles. The reality may change, but the morals are eternal.

Let us address the body of the question and point out a few mistaken assumptions that have no relation at all to the subject under discussion. To begin with, the Talmud never viewed prayer as a ceremony. Rather, prayer in the synagogue is a halakhic obligation. The structure of prayer is not meant to resemble a performance, there is nothing to see, and there are no preferred or less preferred seats. The entire structure of the synagogue broadcasts a message that is the opposite of a ceremonial event.

For example, the chazzan [prayer leader] stands with his back to the congregation, and generally in a lower rather than higher place. The essential part of the prayer service is said by each person silently, while standing. There is no one who leads the prayer, there is only the chazzan whose primary function is to recite the prayer out loud in order to help fulfill the obligation of one who does not know how to pray or is not familiar with the text. In practice, prayer is an act of inner contemplation by which a person connects

---

[7] Jewish law. The word *halakhah* literally implies "the way" – it is the guide for a Jew's day-to-day life.

with his G-d. Therefore any talk of the seating plan, of who is next to whom, gender, status, etc. is foreign to the essence of prayer. It is not a social gathering of any sort. Originally, the tallit[8] [which some women insist on wearing] had no connection to prayer, nor was the reading of the Torah connected to the prayer itself, and certainly not the sermons.

Therefore this entire discussion has no relevance to Jewish sources. It is true that public prayer has developed into different formats, but this is a social phenomenon, not a halakhic one, and this is not what we are discussing.

Q. "I heard a lecture from an activist in one of the women's organizations - a religious woman! - on the subject of supposed discrimination against women in the Talmud. She said that a woman whose husband refuses to give her a document of divorce (a *get*) can remain "chained" to her husband for years if he wishes to spite her by taking negative advantage of the situation..."

True, this can happen – but does such a scenario have any place in Judaism? Can there be a situation where one person intentionally inflicts harm upon another and society accepts this? The entire situation from the outset

---

[8] Prayer shawl

is not Jewish, and is far from any type of behavior root-ed in our sources. In the Talmud we find that one whom the judges ruled is obligated to give his wife a divorce document and does not do so, may not remain part of the community for even a single day.

I once asked a *Dayan* (Jewish court judge) of the Supreme Rabbinical Court if there are solutions for the questions posed by women's groups on the subject. His reply was something to this effect: "There certainly are. I would withhold food from one who refuses to give his wife a *get*, and I guarantee you that within a few hours the *get* would be in her hands." What is preventing this? It is the modern laws, the courts that sanctify the man's rights over the woman's rights. Is his act of intentionally keeping her chained any less severe than withholding food from him for a few hours? Does such a cruel act not justify preventing anyone who is able to bring about the giving of the *get* from leaving the country? If this is modern ethics, it is very far from the way of the Torah.

Q. "What is your view on subjects that have recently made headlines, such as women singing and the modesty of dress demanded of a woman? Why does the Talmud prohibit a good-looking woman from wearing revealing clothing, rather than demanding that men control their desires? ... Why such discrimination?"

This is a good example of a question rooted in ignorance, for which you are not to be blamed. The Talmud does not discuss the manner in which a woman should dress – there is no chapter in the Talmud and not a single tractate that deals directly with women's apparel or the prohibition against displaying herself in one manner or another, having her voice heard, etc. Rather, the Talmud discusses the prohibitions on the male in these matters. Regarding relationships between a man and woman who are not married to each other, the limitations apply to each of them equally. But when it comes to men's sensitivities, the Talmud speaks directly to the men and not to the women. There is nothing wrong with a woman singing or dancing; it is the man who is required to maintain a distance from anything that will cause him spiritual harm or cause him to transgress. Does the fact that a man may not look at an immodestly dressed woman who is not his wife, or even one who is fully dressed for that matter, discriminate against her in any way? Is this offensive to her in any way? This question too stems from modern life phenomena that are, for some reason, assumed to be the obvious ideal lifestyle.

A few years ago I heard an interview with singer Etti Ankry when she was beginning to take on observant Judaism. The interviewer noted that he fears there will come a day when her observance will prevent her from performing. When she asked him why, he answered 'because it will be forbidden for men to attend your concerts.' She replied: 'But women will be allowed, are they nothing in your eyes? To appear before half the world and more is called to stop performing?'

And I would add, has song lost all meaning, is it dependent only on an audience, on money, on honor, publicity and career - things that have no connection whatsoever to song and music? Are we not trying to understand our traditional sources through a new set of assumptions, from a world whose value system is radically different from that of the Talmud?

Of course, once Chazal[9] established guidelines for what is prohibited for a man, it would not be proper for a woman not to be sensitive to the laws that apply to him. But this has nothing at all to do with whether or not he is able to "control" his desires. These laws were established for all men as one framework, and are obligatory upon everyone regardless of their sensitivities. Therefore, just as it is forbidden to smoke in public areas because there are people whom it disturbs, so too it is not proper to dress in public in a manner that may disturb others, or in a manner that will not be respectful towards other people or towards the woman herself.

We are not necessarily speaking here about their

---

[9] Chazal is an acronym for the Hebrew *Chachameinu Zichronam Livracha* – our Sages of Blessed Memory. The name Chazal generally refers to Jewish Sages who lived during the period when the Mishnah and Talmud were written, beginning some 2,000 years ago during the latter part of the Second Temple period and continuing beyond the onset of the Exile, for approximately 300 years.

desires, but about their ability to follow the halakhah. From here, indirectly, stem the laws pertaining to societal norms, which actually pertain to laws between man and his fellow man.

Regarding a married woman, in addition to the requirement of modesty in public, there is the issue of loyalty to her husband. Modesty has value for a person himself, but this concept is not limited to women. There is also the matter of a woman's natural inner feeling of modesty, something which as a man, I of course do not understand. Women say that modesty for them is a necessity, that dressing immodestly and sharing something personal with strange people is embarrassing. In the Talmud we find that one who simply removes a woman's head covering must pay a heavy penalty for the shame he has caused her. Why do all women not feel shame when exposing themselves? I don't know; perhaps the general societal erosion influences and detracts from the natural feeling of modesty.

The Chief Rabbi of Jerusalem, one of the leading halakhic authorities of his generation, Harav Zvi Pesach Frank, had a neighbor who was a singer. From inside his home he was able to hear her singing and practicing. Many would come to him seeking answers, advice, or to pray in the daily prayer service held in his home. He was once asked: "Perhaps the Rav should ask her not to sing out loud, after all, the Talmud says that a woman's singing must not be heard by men." The Rav responded: "Do I have the right to tell someone what to do in his own home? Is it not her privilege? The most I can do is to ask her, perhaps, to be considerate during prayer times..." His Shulchan Arukh[10] was the same one followed by everyone else, containing not a single halakhah that he did not take seriously, but he was familiar with it in its entirety.

Q. "... And something else regarding the structure of the man-woman relationship in Jewish law. Is it true that according to Jewish law, a wedding implies that a man has acquired his wife? Is the wife an object, her husband's property? If so, this is outrageous"...

Certainly not – a woman is not an object that her husband owns, and she is not a monetary acquisition or anything of the sort. Can he now sell her to the highest bidder? Can she return the wedding ring and thereby be considered no longer married? Not at all! May he act towards her in any way he wishes as if she is his monetary acquisition? Certainly not! And the list goes on - there is no comparison between marriage and acquiring an object.

---

[10] the authoritative Code of Jewish Law

Q. "...My friend showed me the opening pages of the Talmudic tractate that discusses weddings, and it is written there, "a woman is acquired in one of three ways." The terminology of acquisition implies that the covenant between a man and woman, their deep bonds, are nothing more than a section in the laws of acquisitions"...

1) The concept of acquisition in the language of our Sages has a completely different meaning than its usage in modern Hebrew, and here lies the source of the mistake in your question. Chazal's understanding of acquisition is of a symbolic act that expresses intent and resolve regarding a particular action. Any change in status, any creation of halakhic-legal status, requires an action; words alone are not sufficient. "Words in the heart – thoughts – have no validity[11]" because they often end up with, "I meant something else, I didn't say that, etc." However, an objective action, something absolute, puts an end to all uncertainties and deliberations, and takes effect in no uncertain terms.

The performance of a symbolic act grants validity. For example, when a person appoints an agent on his behalf, and did so with a "formal act of acquisition," the agency has greater validity. When a person promises something after having performed what is called

---

[11] See Tractate *Kiddushin* page 49b.

a *kinyan,* his obligation is that much greater. This is not an act of purchasing, but rather one of appointing. No one acquired anything from anyone, even though in modern Hebrew the word *kinyan* sounds that way. In short, the mistake is based on a wrong understanding of the Hebrew.

2. There are opinions among the authorities that the notion of acquisition does apply to a woman, but not at all in the commercial usage. Rather, it refers to the idea of her being designated only to him. In other words, in laws pertaining to marriage, she is "his" and not another man's; she is a married woman. He does not own her, nor may his friend borrow her even if all parties consent. It is a *halakhic* status.

Q. "...There are some things in the *chupah* [marriage canopy] ceremony that bother me greatly. For example: What is this non-reciprocal structure? Why does he say to her, "you are sanctified to me," but she does not say the same to him?"

Judaism does not claim to be equal in the symmetrical sense. It recognizes the differences between a man and a woman, and they are many, in body and in soul. This situation is not dependent on a given time period, the public atmosphere, or the scientific/

judicial/social community. When a man leads the marriage proceedings, when he sanctifies the woman, when he is active and she is passive, he is in effect taking responsibility. The Torah specifically placed the responsibility of maintaining the relationship on the man. The Torah views him as the leader, the one to deal with difficulties, the one to ensure proper maintenance of this system from all perspectives. Even courting, creating the bond, and sustaining it is incumbent on the man; he is the one who is supposed to "search for what he lost [in the imagery of the Sages]."

The marriage ceremony includes the man's giving of a *ketubah*[12] to his bride. This obligates him, as soon as the marriage takes effect, to a list of responsibilities vis-a-vis his wife in all possible areas. He is obligated to support her, relate to her with sensitivity, care for her in all situations, and fulfill all her needs. This includes redeeming her from captivity, caring for her when she is ill, and even taking care of her funeral arrangements, G-d forbid. Every possible scenario is taken into account, including the obligation to maintain the bonds between them. If for whatever reason the bond is broken, he is obligated to continue to sustain her, to make sure she has a place to live, and more.

---

[12] A ketubah is a Jewish marriage contract. Considered an integral part of a Jewish marriage, it outlines the rights and responsibilities of the groom in relation to the bride.

Q. "In one of your Talmud lectures you discussed the structure of the *ketubah*. You asked why in the Torah, the woman has all the privileges and the man has all the obligations. Perhaps I did not understand you correctly or I got mixed up, but I think you said something of that nature"...

It is true that by the *halakhah* "favors" the woman in releasing her from much responsibility and placing many burdens upon the man. However, the woman also has obligations, which stem primarily from her unique essence as a woman. Perhaps because these obligations are part of her nature, they do not need to be anchored in writing as is the case with the man. It could be that this is the result of the load placed upon the woman naturally, and her more delicate, sensitive, and sometimes vulnerable nature. The Torah and Chazal therefore established clear laws to make sure she is not taken advantage of, and to prevent the husband from shirking his responsibility and possibly neglecting her.

While it may be the case that today many women are financially independent, this is their choice; not every woman chooses this path. At times this choice may come at the expense of other things that are important to her. The Torah and Chazal gave women many privileges because they felt the need to protect them and advance them and their needs. They freed women from responsibilities that might be too taxing. It is forbidden to burden a woman with tasks that are contrary to her nature. The Sages of the Medrash explain that "the harsh labor" which the Jewish people endured in Egypt referred to men's work performed by women and vice versa. Clearly this has no connection with physical demands, for otherwise it would be unidirectional, i.e., a problem only for women. The reference here is to the psychological difficulty of performing work for which one is not suited.

Q. "Why is a woman disqualified from serving as a witness? Is she only half a person? Why is she not relied upon? And what about this thing of female rabbis - why can't a woman issue *halakhic* rulings"?

There are situations where women in fact may testify, but the underlying principle is that women are *exempt* from the obligation to testify. Testifying is primarily an obligation, not a privilege. Giving testimony can be emotionally taxing. The witness must endure a difficult interrogation and cross-examination, at times under oath, and must withstand the tension of the court's interrogation. This may at times be difficult, demanding that he recall minute details in the presence of other witnesses who contradict his testimony, as well as difficult litigants.

There is no correlation between the severity of the matter and the woman's suitability to testify. There can be capital cases where she may testify and minor monetary cases in which she may not testify. The Torah mainly exempted the woman from obligatory testimony, from the difficulty of having to contend with criminal matters.

There may possibly be another reason why the Torah says that a woman should not testify. This is not an iron-clad rule, but in general, creativity, imagination, and intuition (the "right lobe") are more developed in the woman. In general this is an advantage, though when it comes to the need for precise, factual and technical testimony, this is a disadvantage. Therefore, when the community recognizes a particular woman as highly suited for a particular task and is willing to offer her the position, according to Tosafot she may be appointed for the position. I am not relating here to what is practiced today.

Regarding the question of women issuing halakhic rulings, the question is purely theoretical and has no connection to the subject of gender. While there are women today with a very impressive amount of knowledge, thank G-d, the difference between their knowledge and that required of one who issues halakhic rulings is vast, and there is no comparison, as we all know. There are many men with broad knowledge of Judaism, and there are women who know much more than them, and they teach Judaism most

impressively. But in today's reality, there are no wom-
en with the amount of knowledge that comes near
that which is required for a Halakhic decisor.

Q. "Perhaps since all the *halakhic* decisors are
men, their rulings tend to favor the men"?

The approach inherent in this question is based on
a world that is not at all familiar with the concept of
poskim[13] and the world of *halakhah*. The subject of personal biases and *halakhic* rulings is something I will
have to address separately, because this requires the
breaking of many stigmas that stem from ignorance.

But to get to the point: First, is there a contradiction
between what is good for men and what is good for
women? Secondly, your assumptions are wrong. On
the contrary, it appears from Chazal that it is the wom-
en who are favored more than the men. For example,
the structure of the ketubah consists of a list of obligations that a man has towards his wife. Accordingly,
throughout my years of married life, I have essentially said to my wife: "Don't go out to work to support
the family, go out to work only if you believe that this
is right for you." This is not a matter of generosity or
over-stringency; this is the Jewish law. The obligation
to support the family is the husband's. The woman

---

[13] Issuers of *halakhic* rulings

may go out to work in research or the arts, she may go to a dance course, learn Chinese medicine, and visit museums, as long as the house functions while the husband goes out to work.

Unpleasant confrontations with an office clerk, the need to testify in court, all sorts of unpleasant encounters – the woman is exempt from all these; they are the man's obligation. In the words of Psalms (45:14): "All the glory of the King's daughter is within" – this encapsulates Chazal's guidelines for the woman – she is the daughter of King. She does not need to impinge upon her honor with outside confrontations. It is her right to remain within her kingdom and not to be involved in interrogations, inquiries and negotiations. And what is Cherem d'Rabbenu Gershom[14] if not for the purpose of protecting women? There are hundreds of references in the Talmud that are the polar opposite of the claim inherent in the question.

Q. "My cousin became a baal teshuva [newly-observant Jew] and never misses a single prayer service in the synagogue, zealously. I told him that for this reason alone I would never become a baalat teshuva. He answered that women are

---

[14] an enactment by Rabbeinu Gershom about 1,000 years ago that a man may not marry more than one woman at a time, or divorce his wife without her consent.

exempt from time-dependent mitzvot anyway.[15]
What does this mean? Are women second-
class? Why do women have fewer mitzvot
[commandments]? Are the men holier?"

You asked and provided the answer simultane-
ously. There are matters that are not suitable for the
natural life of a woman, and there are matters that a
woman has no need for at all.

The exemption from time-dependent mitzvot, according to Rabbi Shimshon Rafael Hirsch zt"l[16], one
of the great *halakhic* authorities in Germany in the
19th century, belong in the former grouping. Jewish
law exempts women from the majority of commandments that are time-dependent. For example, a mother of small children does not need to pray three times
a day. It is not appropriate for a woman whose child
wishes to nurse "right now" to have to say to the
child: "The sun is setting in ten minutes, I need to first
pray Mincha and then I will nurse you." Nor, after a
night of nursing, should a woman be pressured to recite the *Sh'ma*[17] before a specific time in the morning.

---

[15] Women are exempt from the vast majority of positive Torah commandments that
are time-dependent, such as eating in the sukkah on the festival of Sukkot. There are
some exceptions, such as the obligation to eat matzah on the first night of Passover,
as well as all laws relating to the Sabbath, which women are obligated to fulfill.
[16] This stands for zecher tzaddik livracha, meaning "a righteous man of blessed
memory."
[17] The three paragraphs beginning with the word Sh'ma – acceptance of the yoke of the
Kingdom of Heaven. This prayer must be recited twice daily: once in the morning
before a quarter of the day has passed, and once in the evening after nightfall.

The prayer ambience is different for a man than for a woman. If a woman wishes to pray, why should she need to do so specifically with a *minyan*,[18] when in fact the trees in the forest, the meeting point of the sky and the sea, the desert, a cloud, can provide her with much greater inspiration for prayer? Prayer is an expression of emotions; how can a woman be demanded to express her emotions right here and now? I, for example, as a man, have a greater need for such a structure. There are times when I realized how much I needed to pray only *after* I finished, precisely when I had thought it was not a good time for me. The structure brings me back to myself and to Hashem.

Perhaps your cousin, being a man, has an easier time with structure? Perhaps this *halakhah* corresponds precisely to people's nature? While this is certainly a generalization, there is something to the fact that for the majority of women, the connection to their inner self does not require any outside assistance, such as structure or a push. This is not the case when it comes to men.

Men tend to love the study of Gemara more than women, specifically its intricate details, calculations, and analysis. The Torah and Chazal in general grant women a much higher spiritual status; they believe that she is able to reach spiritual heights with much less need for structure. Let us take the example of the

---

[18] A minimum of ten adult Jewish males; this is the required quorum for communal men's prayer. Certain parts of the service may only be recited in the presence of a minyan, and praying with a minyan has an elevated status in general.

first mitzvah of the Torah: *"Be fruitful and multiply"* – only men are commanded, while women are exempt from this mitzvah. Is there a practical way to fulfill the mitzvah without a woman? Certainly not! However, according to one explanation, a woman has such a strong desire to bring children into the world that she need not be commanded to do so, for she would fulfill it on her own even with the great difficulty and would withstand the suffering that many men would not be able to endure.

Furthermore, did you ever stop to think that Devorah the Prophetess - a judge over the Jewish nation, the great poet whom the Bible places upon a pedestal – serves as a model to teach us that there are no gender limitations when it comes to attaining spiritual heights? We find in Tanna D'vei Eliyahu (chapter 9): "Heaven and earth are my witnesses that the Divine Spirit rests upon everyone, whether man, woman, male slave, or maidservant, corresponding to his actions." The Rambam cites this in his opus on Jewish Law.

We see that a woman apparently has less need for structure in order to attain lofty heights. However, the levels attained through Torah study cannot be acquired without toiling in Torah with extreme devotion, which is not suited for most women. In our generation, a large portion of the men are not suited for this either. I have taught in both men's and women's schools, I am aware of the reality of the situation.

The reason it is so rare to find a woman who can be categorized as a *Talmid Chacham* (Torah scholar) is that there are not many women who are suited for and wish to dedicate themselves to such an exhausting and demanding course of Torah study. If we were to find such a G-d- fearing woman, however, I do not believe that there would be any objection whatsoever. There were a few such women in history and no one objected. However in our day the question is completely theoretical, given the general decline in the level of dedication to any area on the part of both genders.

I conclude this chapter by describing my personal feelings upon reading chapters in the Bible. The Torah conveys a strong message regarding woman's decisive and leading role in our lives, even from behind the scenes – all in accordance with her nature. In the book of B'reshit (Genesis) – the book of the forefathers – the influential ones are always the women: Eve (Chavah), Sarah (about whom G-d said to Avraham: *"Whatever Sarah tells you, heed her voice[19]"*), Hagar, Rivka in her handling of the strife between Yaakov and Esav, Rachel, and Leah. We can apply this to Devorah and her Chief of Staff Barak, and many other instances.

Following in this path, Chazal magnify our image of Miriam as one of the three leaders of the nation in its formation, and underscore the role of the women

---

[19] Genesis 21:12.

who did not despair of entering the Land of Israel. This is what emerges from almost every chapter of the Talmud, until finally Admon, one of the Sages of the Mishnah, shouts out in complaint about Chazal's preferential treatment of women: "Just because I'm a male I should lose out?!"[20]

---

[20] Tractate *Baba Batra* 139b.

CHAPTER 3

INTELLIGENT, PRETTY, GOOD-HEARTED, BUT...

Hi Meir,

You know who I am but I'm not sure whether you know me by name. I'm Avner, I participate in the Yemima workshop in HaMakom on the day that you give your class. We occasionally exchange a few words. I wanted to share with you something that is probably absolutely terrible, from your standpoint, but for me, it's fantastic – and this difference between us is exactly what underscores that which bothers me so much.

I recently met a young woman, and I can't even begin to describe how she is exactly what I always dreamt of. She's smart, witty, talented, altruistic and sensitive. She also volunteers for some really good causes. I admit that when I first saw her, I mainly saw how beautiful she was– look, that's what everyone who meets her first notices – but as I gradually got to know her, I realized that she's not just a "regular" girl; she is truly a special person. It's really going well between us, and the relationship is definitely headed in a good direction.

Last week she tells me that she has something important to share with me, and that she's a bit afraid to say it. I wondered, does she want to tell me she has another boyfriend? Or maybe that she has some terrible sickness? Then she starts shooting off all sorts of questions about Judaism: "What is Judaism for you? How do you feel about it?" Questions like that. I couldn't figure out where she got this all of a sudden, why she's interested in this now, and what it has to do with that scary thing she wants to tell me. I told her that Judaism doesn't really concern me that much, I never thought about it too seriously, and I'm not religious. So she says, "Hold on tight, I have to tell you the truth: My father is Jewish, but my mother is not." She said they got married in Russia where things like that weren't important. Her mother's parents are the same – the father is Jewish, the mother is not.

I didn't understand why she was making a big deal of this. So only her father is Jewish – half a Jew, a quarter-Jew, what difference does it make? She said that she checked with a few religious people who told her that according to Jewish Law she is not considered Jewish.

I asked her, "Since when does Jewish Law concern you so much?" and she answered, "It doesn't bother me, but I thought that perhaps it would bother you, you know, in the future ... maybe... the subject of children, but if it doesn't bother you then I'm fine." That was the end of the discussion.

I then told a few of my friends about this, and they said to me: "What? Don't you have any boundaries? You're not normal! Just leave her!" I actually believe that there's no problem with mixing different cultures, and that it actually brings more peace in the world. I don't look at the nationality, but at the person; I see nothing wrong with that. So they said to me, "If you marry her, you might as well not come to the synagogue on Yom Kippur, you're just making a mockery of it." She is even willing to come with me to the synagogue, to pray, and fast. She loves Jewish customs, and besides that, her father is Jewish, so it's not as if she has no connection at all to Judaism.

I thought perhaps you could explain the problem to me on a slightly deeper level than what I've been hearing from my friends. And if you can, write whether the Torah itself states that this is forbidden, and where it is written – assuming it is a source accessible to someone like me.

Thank you very much,
Avner

Hi Avner,

Of course I know you! You forgot that we once had a long talk on the steps with Evyatar Banai and some young musicians he was working with? You told me about an ancient Chinese song of the sea. (You'll remember – you're younger than me!)

Listen to this interesting coincidence: Just this morning I met a man, a rabbi in a Lubavitch community in Ukraine. He told me that every Shabbat afternoon they have a Hassidic gathering, with a light meal and quiet, moving songs that touch the soul, leading into the night when Shabbat ends. And he told me that every week there's a nice Jew with a long white beard who joins them and sits there in his Hassidic garb – and spends the entire time crying. Everyone's singing, and he's just crying the whole time. The Lubavitcher said that he once asked him if everything is OK at home and with his life in general. The man answered: "Everything is fine - and nothing is fine. When I was younger and didn't know a thing about Judaism, I married a Gentile – and as a result, my kids are all Gentiles, and I have lost my continuation in the People of Israel."

I asked the Lubavitcher who was telling me this story, "Maybe there's a way they can convert, because of the special circumstances? Did you check?" He said, "In general, we Lubavitchers stay away from that, we don't initiate conversions."

Avner, what's really hard for me in your story is that you don't seem to be aware of the whole picture, not do you understand all the ramifications. So first let me say: If you want to know how this plays out according to Judaism, and what's the source for not marrying out, it's clearly written in Deuteronomy 7: "Do not marry them..." But Maimonides, in his Halakhic magnum opus called Mishne Torah, adds some very strong and sharp words of explanation – because he wants to go beyond just the specific act of marrying out; he relates to the entire national, historic context. He writes that the reason this prohibition is so severe is because it means the uprooting and destruction of one's most basic bonds with Judaism and the Jewish People. Marriage, and everything that leads up to it, is the entry ticket to our national pedigree. You can of course ask why we need nations altogether, and what's wrong with a global world, and the like – but that's for a different discussion[21]. In terms of Judaism, there's no question that our nationhood is commonly passed down through our families – and if one marries out, the branch that he represents in our extended national family will simply be cut off.

I recently stayed in a hotel where I met an elderly resident of Tel Aviv, a Holocaust survivor (one of a diminishing number of survivors entitled to two weeks of hotel vacation each year, I believe as part of the reparations from Germany). This man was over 90 years old, and needed a foreign worker to assist him with his day-to-day functioning.

He was very preoccupied and wanted to hear my opinion on the following question: In all the seven levels of hell that he passed through during the Shoah, he always made sure to carry his small pair of

---

[21] See below.

tefillin with him. He managed to hide them in very unusual ways. While in a labor camp, he would take the tefillin with him to work. The moment the Nazi soldier took a break and stopped watching the prisoners so closely, he would hide behind a tree, quickly don his tefillin, and take them off. At one point his tefillin were found and confiscated.

A group of "new" Jews from a new transport then passed by them. One of them left the line, took out a pair of tefillin, and for some miraculous reason, gave them to him – he has no idea why – and quickly returned to his line. These tefillin ended up being worn not only by him; a long line of Jews formed in the pre-morning hours in their shack, waiting their hurried turn to don the tefillin. The man says he believes that it was the merit of the tefillin that ultimately saved him.

After the war, he resided in Warsaw until he was able to attain a certificate to move to the Land of Israel. He had some business acumen, but there was a destitute Jew in Warsaw who would ask him every day to let him don his tefillin. When he left Poland, he decided to leave the tefillin to the poor man, thinking that he would soon be able purchase a new pair for himself - but how would the poor man be able to procure tefillin in Warsaw? And so it was; upon arrival in the Land of Israel, he bought himself new tefillin.

Today there are people who say to him: "You should have held on to your tefillin, you shouldn't have given them away, they are not just any old object, but were with you during the difficult years, they're a part of history." The man feels that on the other hand he gave someone the opportunity to perform a mitzvah, and did something charitable. "What do you say," he asks me, "should I have given them to him?"

I replied that of course, he was right to give him the tefillin.

But then I thought to myself: What is troubling this Jew after almost 70 years? Just look at his self-sacrifice to maintain some connection to his Judaism, doing his utmost under such difficult conditions! And this is how Jews held on to their Judaism with great self-sacrifice throughout the generations. Let's assume we can say that it is all ancient and primitive, that this holy tradition has no value and need not be perpetuated, or even that its opposite has great value. Should we not devote a bit of thought and analysis before choosing to take such a fateful step? It's really an irreversible historic decision.

Note that your girlfriend felt what you did not feel, that perhaps there is some sort of problem here, that you might want to take into account that your children won't be Jewish according to Jewish Law. From a historical perspective, there is no framework for Judaism outside of Jewish Law, even for one who does not observe all its details.

Avner, all I'm saying is that it is worth it for you to

meet, either with me or with anyone else you wish, to discuss the subject. In general, before you take such a drastic step regarding your Judaism, why not sit and learn a bit about it, become familiar with it, so as to know whether you are forfeiting something of value. For a person of your intelligence, it would be very strange to make such a decision out of ignorance. Afterwards, you can decide whatever you choose with clear understanding, with open eyes. This is the free choice that every person has.

I believe that the very fact that you sent me this email says that you attach significance to the matter. In the meantime, I will tell you that I believe that the entire world, deep down, thanks the Jewish nation for its existence – for preserving itself, and for presenting a code of conduct and an ethical compass. I'm not referring necessarily to each and every individual, but to the nation as a whole. This is my response to the "world peace" you wrote about. Certainly it is a wonderful and lofty value, but it will not come about by blurring and confusing people's identities.

Regarding the value of belonging to a group, family, community, or nation, and whether they are all similar in essence – let's speak about this in person. This subject is of a wider scope; you are questioning the very principle of division into nations, which does not relate only to Judaism. In my view, just as I have close family and an extended family that provide me with stability, an anchor, a connection and a sense of belonging, so too I feel a connection to my nation – albeit a different type of connection.

Even on the simplest level, there exists team spirit and pride in one's group in many areas: Golani Brigade soldiers believe they are the elite unit of the Israel Defense Forces, just as the paratroopers believe the same about themselves. One who says, "I love all nations equally" is like a married man who says, "I love all women equally." Such a man apparently does not really love anyone.

Regarding the Jewish people's mission in the world – the obligation and responsibility to be a model for social justice, high ethics, love and optimism – this is a matter for a lengthy discussion. Similarly, regarding the Jewish nation's obligation to elevate and refine the entire world, as indeed happened throughout history – we can speak about this when we meet.

If all of this sounds like nonsense given today's reality – this may explain the questions you raised in your letter. When we are not true to our task, we begin to lose our confidence in the uniqueness of the Jewish people. This may indeed be the source of the questions you raised in this letter.

Hoping to see you soon,
Meir

CHAPTER 4

WHAT IS EASIER – TO BE RELIGIOUS, OR SECULAR?

... Meir,

it's not easy for me to say this, but I find the daily prayers to be a restricting burden and an irritating chore. What's all this mumbling? Isn't it enough to attend a ceremony in the synagogue once a week, on Friday or the Sabbath? Why must a religious person go through this ritual every day? ...

Alex

Dear Alex,

One time during my army service, I entered an office to arrange something. The young soldier at the desk told me that she's from a totally secular family, she knows nothing about Judaism, but she had been told that she descends from a great Rabbi. "I believe his name is Rabbi Kook," she said. "There is such a person, right? And also a Rabbi Raanan [his son-in-law – ed.], we're also related to him."

I was curious: "How are you related?" She didn't know: "We're distant relatives, I guess, but I have no idea. It also doesn't interest me too much." She then asked me: "Tell the truth, no one is listening: Don't you ever have the urge to be like us, even just for a short time, to enjoy life like a secular person, to be unrestricted, to do whatever comes your way?"

I was young, self-righteous, and argumentative, and in typical Jewish fashion I answered with a question: "Why don't you tell **me** the truth: Have you never had the urge to be like one of those religious girls, without the restrictions of a secular person?"
Surprised, she responded: "What restrictions? What can't I do?"
I said: "To pray, for example – don't you ever have the desire to pray, to really pray?"

Allow me to digress for a moment from the story of our conversation to say that at times I feel an inner storm, with everything bellowing inside me and I don't know where to turn. One feeling or another surges and rises above the surface, but I feel that I can't express it without negating it. Can I relate it to anyone in the world, to express it precisely as it is, without any alterations, without embellishing or worrying about what others may say, without feeling disappointment that people cannot truly understand each other because each person is different?

How many people are able to forge a relationship of such closeness with someone that they can say they have found a true "soul-mate," even in phys-ical-world terms? Is there such a connection that is always, always open, without a single moment of separation? And even if one is fortunate and has one to whom he can tell anything, that person is not always available, and it's not always smart to tell him everything as it is, and not everything can be said, and there are things I just don't know how to say. It is so complex ... Where can I go to simply shout out, quietly or out loud, that which is screaming deep inside me? Where can I sing my deepest song, and know that there is One who is not only listening, but is waiting to hear me?

For me, my army service, wherever I may have been located, for regular service or reserve duty, was a time for my "innermost" feelings – productive and deep, with emotions swaying from one extreme to the other. You find yourself close to nature, close to the sunrise and the sunset, to the panoramic views, to the stars of the night. You're totally cut off from the day-to-day routine, from protective family and community. You're with friends and worlds that are distant and enriching, things you never meet so intensively, with an openness of heart not found in civilian life.

It may have been the military assignments, the locations, or the thoughts about the situation that aroused this. At times I literally "lived" just from prayer to prayer. Some of my prayers were such strong expressions, with faith that is so strong and tangible that the hopes, the yearnings, and the words of the prayers were stronger even than the desired results.

There were times when I would stand opposite the

sea or mountains, on Friday evening at the onset of the Sabbath, reciting *Kabbalat Shabbat*,[22] either alone or with others, and the vision of "more than the roars of many waters, mightier than the waves of the sea, You are mighty on high, G-d"[23] – was so vivid that it had long jumped out from the pages of the prayer book into the endless expanse of the Divine Presence. There was a holiness that you could feel with your hands.

There were difficult times, filled with loneliness, when I would sneak out for a minute or two – or an hour or two, if there was enough time – for a moment of prayer. I'd be standing opposite the Source of beauty, the Source of love, the Source of joy and all that is good, pouring out my innermost sensations before Him. I would return from these occasions all cleansed, with a feeling of purity that permeated every part of my body, with a pleasant lightness, love, and connection to everything.

Back to my conversation: I was unable to describe all this then, and I did not tell her all this, but I did describe a small part of the unique ability to express one's deepest emotions through prayer. I asked her: "Do you never feel the need to pray? Did you ever want to pray but then you say, 'It's too awkward… What am I, a religious fanatic? Have I become a *baalat*

---

[22] A prayer ceremony welcoming the Sabbath Queen. Often sung aloud, it consists of a set of psalms, followed by a song known as Lecha Dodi, followed by two more psalms.
[23] A verse from the second psalm that follows Lecha Dodi (Psalm 93:4).

teshuva?[24] People will mock me that I'll soon start wearing skirts and throwing stones at cars driving on the Sabbath...'[25] So it turns out," I told her, "that you're actually quite restricted, and can't allow yourself to do everything I can do; isn't that so?"

Quite surprised, she remarked that she had never thought about it from that perspective: "All I knew was that Judaism was just a bunch of things that you're not allowed to do..."

In my youth, I spent a short time studying in the Yeshiva in Kfar Chassidim[26] – a non-Hassidic-style Yeshiva patterned after the *musar* movement.[27] It provided a very pleasant atmosphere, and had I been able to, I would have remained there for many more years. During the month of Elul, when yeshiva environments typically focus on preparing for the High Holydays, there was an atmosphere of tension, a type of pressure. I had a hard time with this. I searched for the writings of Rabbi Kook; he has a different approach. His books were listed in the catalog, but I couldn't find any in the library.

The yeshiva's Mashgiach - director of educational/spiritual matters - was Rabbi Dov Yaffe: not a young man, gentle and pleasant in an extraordinarily unusual manner[28]. He is a product of the *musar* movement,

---

[24] A baal teshuva is a formerly secular Jew who adopts a religious lifestyle. Baalat teshuva is the feminine form.
[25] A common libel disseminated against hareidi Jews
[26] A small village in northern Israel.
[27] The word musar refers to ethics or moral conduct. The musar movement sought to advance the teaching of Jewish ethics and morals.
[28] He died after this letter was written, in 2017.

and it is apparent from his every move how much effort he put into character development and self-control. He is a man full of light and goodness. At times, I would imagine that this is how Rabbi Kook looked and spoke – full of optimism, with a constant smile as if whispering a secret, seeing only the beauty in everything and everyone. I asked him whether the Yeshiva had Rabbi Kook's book on prayer, *Olat Reiyah*. He answered, "I know that we had it, but it looks like the zealots got hold of it [it is well-known that there were those who opposed Rabbi Kook's worldview]. If you don't find it in the Yeshiva library, ask so-and-so, he may have it in his house." He then added, "But you know, there are other books on prayer, books that are easier to understand, more basic. Rabbi Kook was a great kabbalist and not everyone is able to understand him. Did you ever hear of the book *Olat Tamid*? It is an excellent book explaining the words of prayers, written by a very special man named Rabbi Huminer."

"I haven't heard of the book," I answered, "I'll look for it." And so I did, but I added, "Rabbi Kook's books contain something that other books do not, even if one does not understand what he has in mind. They have a unique aura." I did not know then how to define it, perhaps not even today. At a later stage, when I read parts of the introduction to *Olat Reiyah*, I understood that a sentence such as "Prayer for us and for the entire world is an absolute necessity, and is also the most kosher[29] of pleasures" I would not find in any book explaining the words of prayer, even in the best of these books.

So here I am, using my own words and experience to tell this young female soldier, a member of Rabbi Kook's family, what he wrote to her and to others along the way, about prayer being the greatest and best pleasure that one can experience, of all the pleasures of this world.

I would like, in addition, to address the Torah commandment to pray. Prayer, in essence, is a personal expression of feeling. Every conversation with G-d is a prayer; it makes no difference what you say. In the language of the Torah, prayer is called "service of the heart." The text that was established during the period of the Second Temple is meant to assist us. You stand before an Omnipotent infinite power, the ultimate perfection of everything, and you wish to concentrate, to express with precision, not forget any important item, to properly direct your thoughts – pretty difficult. The Sages therefore authored a text that can help us express ourselves, a basic text upon which one may then add whatever he wishes. But the most important element of prayer, according to Jewish Law as well, is the connection between the heart and the mouth, and not an external series of words.

---

[29] Rav Kook used the Hebrew word for "kosher," meaning here legitimate, appropriate, and even powerful.

If one finds that he can spend ten minutes praying with very deep concentration, but loses it when
praying for forty minutes, the short prayer is generally preferred, the one where he can pour his heart out.
Devoted prayer of this type also takes precedence
over praying in a *minyan*[30] or in the synagogue[31], according to many authorities. This is the main principle, without getting into the details of the law.

But this is not sufficient. Even service of the heart
requires a framework. Let's say you're running
around in the middle of the day, and the last thing
that fits into your schedule right then is to pray.
Suddenly you notice that there are only ten minutes
until sunset – the end of the time for the afternoon
service[32]. So you drop everything, leave, and go to
pray – just because of the demands of the structure of
the law. Fifteen minutes later you return to the same
things – but from a totally different place; you feel
flowing, high, purposeful. You then realize that this
truly was what you needed most at that time: prayer.
The structure gives us balance. Thank you, our Sages,
for giving us the text and structure.

Because you asked about prayer, I responded about
the yoke of prayer as compared to the enjoyment it
brings. But actually, it is a good idea to view each and every commandment from its internal perspective as well.

---

[30] A *minyan* is the quorum of ten required for communal prayer.
[31] Synagogue prayer is generally preferred over prayer outside a synagogue, such as in one's home.
[32] The Afternoon Service - Mincha - may be recited from half an hour after midday until sunset.

Don't be afraid to write back freely and critically.
-Meir

CHAPTER 5

AND PERHAPS FAITH IS ALL JUST AN ILLUSION?

Dear Meir,

... I completed my army service a year ago, and then I spent six months in India. I found myself a few times in Chabad Houses, mainly on weekends and for Friday night meals. The people there were nice; they were always talking about Judaism and offering me to put on tefillin. When I returned to Israel, I looked for a place in Tel Aviv that would give me some Judaism, without pressure. Your classes are really good.

I have a question, and I hope I'm not over-philosophizing. I'm generally a believing person, and I see it's good for me, especially during hard times. I've even found myself sometimes actually talking to G-d, asking for His help. But sometimes I think: "Maybe faith in G-d is just an illusion, a way to fool ourselves in order to make life more comfortable? Maybe man made up the existence of G-d for his own needs?" This is a depressing thought, because if there's truly nothing absolute, then I'm simply living a convenient lie. Maybe it's just easier to believe that someone is taking care of you and that you always have someone to turn to, even if in reality it's all made-up. But then sometimes I think the opposite: "That's baloney! Of course there exists a Supreme Force!"

If you have something to tell me about these thoughts, I would love to read it, or you can call me on my cell.

Thanks in advance,

Gil

Shalom Gil.

You're always welcome; never worry about raising "too-philosophical" questions. Take a deep breath, because my answer will also be philosophical – like yours – and long, too.

Rebbe Nachman of Breslov writes a lot that even doubts play a role in one's faith. Faith in G-d is just like relations between people – sometimes very close and loving, and at other times distant and uncertain. With G-d, too, we sometimes don't strongly feel His providence, His closeness and His love. On occasion, people who are close, even a husband and wife, get angry and yell - but when this happens, it doesn't at all mean that their relationship is over; both sides know that closeness comes with ups and downs.

Sometimes a person asks himself, as the Israelites did in the wilderness, "Is G-d in our midst, or not?" Perhaps it's just a human invention? Or perhaps He does exist, but not as one who hears us and pays attention? And perhaps sometimes we feel one way and differently at other times? Or maybe we should just categorize it as "uncertain" – as in (my understanding of) the classic Poem for a Weekday by the Israeli poet Rachel Shapira[33]: The lover asks plaintively: "Are you responding? Are you

answering me?... Perhaps my life's rhythm pulsates in your ears as well... perhaps you are like me after all[34], for in your face is suddenly reflected mine."

Yes, there are doubts – but who says we must fear them, or come to conclusions based on them? For at other times, we will actually feel very close to G-d, as if we are seeing Him with our eyes, burning up from love for Him. Our feelings, our deepest relationships – they are always a blend of up and downs, of that which is hidden and that which is open, of despair and hope.

Faith: A Luxury, or an Essential Basic Product?

Regarding your doubts as to whether mankind might have invented the concept of belief in G-d: Let's assume that mankind did invent it – why did he do so? The answer is that this is what mankind needs: to know that there is a beginning and a purpose. We cannot live with the sensation that nothing

---

[33] The poem is ostensibly a love song of closeness and distance, and of the lover's hopeful longing for her partner to recognize the great efforts she makes for him in many details of everyday life. The poem poignantly asks: "Is there mutuality in this relationship? Are you responding to me? Perhaps you are like me, but I do not know enough of what you are experiencing. I yearn for a response, a sign, a hint of our relationship." I believe that this describes the structure of our bonds of faith in G-d.

[34] reminiscent of the Biblical verse, "G-d made man in the image of G-d."

has value, that there is no meaning to what we do, that there is no absolute ethic, no ultimate goal, task, or mission in our lives. It is unbearable to function with the idea that everything will ultimately end up in one place, that there is no soul or continuation, no judge and no judgement, no good or bad. For if G-d is simply a figment of our imagination, then who really decided what is good and what is not? The values promulgated in His name are nothing but mere emotions of compassion and pity, and can vary from person to person. Everything would then be one big piece of despair. No one can exist this way, with feelings that he must always escape and cancel out such thoughts, and with the need to develop artificial optimism and fight against any sign of old age. No one can exist stubbornly marching upstream against nature, fighting hopeless wars, and battling against the fear of death by ignoring it.

(Don't worry; I'm not just repeating your question, though it may seem so; I'm setting up the answer!)

Sometimes, a person is so weak and alone, that he simply cannot go on, psychologically, without a strong and infinite father to whom he can turn, with whom he can speak, and from whom he can seek help. He needs someone with whom he can feel safe, knowing that there is someone above him looking after him and taking charge.

Sometimes a person feels betrayed by his environment, that he has no more strength for wars and no one on whom to depend. And so he searches for a figure that he can trust and believe in completely.

Sometimes a person intuitively rises up against injustice – believing instinctively that beyond all the mediocre human courts of justice and forms of government, there exists some power of absolute truth and source of absolute justice, and that in the end, true justice will be served.

Indeed, sometimes the depression caused by the thought of cessation and death causes one to want to believe that there truly is a real eternity.

There are times when a person stands before the beauty of creation, or the beauty of another person, and his heart expands – but also contracts at the same time, because he lacks the wherewithal to contain this tremendous splendor. He also knows that one day, it will cease to exist for him. He stands helpless – and then understands that this beauty must be just a hint and a taste of an even more complete grandeur.

And thus, facing this goodness that is all so wondrous yet also limited and incomplete, man finds it handy to believe that somewhere, there truly exists perfection, a source that is whole and contains all beauty, wisdom, might, good, kindness, and the like. He finds it comfortable to believe that in the face of frail, impermanent, decaying human love, there actually exists love that is complete, idyllic, and enduring – one that is always full, an inexhaustible source of love: **G-d.**

Now that we know how important this need is, your question again comes to the fore: How can we know that G-d is real, and not just a human invention on which to rely for a more comfortable life?

Must "Human Need" and "Truth" Contradict?

Perhaps the many types of difficulties I provided above have sharpened the question sufficiently so that you realize that the answer is actually embedded within them. Allow me to elaborate, in stages.

Let's assume that man seeks a comfortable life. What's wrong with that? Are we masochists?

Furthermore, we see from all the above that man can simply not live without faith. It is not just something that adds comfort and convenience, but is actually critical for normal human life and man's ability to function, create and not be constantly depressed, weak, and frightened. This force that is imbued in man is critical for our existence. It is our optimism, our confidence that everything will be OK. It is what empowers us to overcome failures, downfalls, mourning and loss. What we call "faith" is the strength to get up every morning anew with optimism, even when there is no rational basis for such. It is the strength to take action on behalf of others, for the sake of future generations that ostensibly are of no interest to us.

What this means is that anyone who has the will to live, or even any semblance of optimism, is a believer. And the more optimistic a person is, the more he believes in G-d. He does not necessarily call the object of his faith "G-d;" he can call it by any name he pleases, but this is just a matter of semantics, not substance.

Everyone has a conscience, a sensation of what is good and what is bad. And it does not only apply to him himself; he will also get angry at others if he feels they are doing something "bad" or unethical. This, too, is every person's "portion of G-d above," the faith that is imbued within each of us. This conscience impedes one's being a "non-believer," and will prevent him from thinking that his deeds in this world have no real significance. The conscience says that there most definitely is meaning to absolute justice, to absolute truth, and to absolute goodness. All this, in one word, is: G-d.

I maintain that every person, deep within himself, believes that he will have some type of existence even after his death. He believes that there is an absolute force, and complete justice, and some type of supervision over the world – and that the world is not merely headed aimlessly towards oblivion. Every person feels this – sometimes more, and sometimes less.

Yet still, we cannot suffice with this – so if you're still with me, let's delve a bit deeper. Jewish faith is not something that exists only in man's thoughts or imagination; it comprises the belief in One True and Absolute G-d as Objective Truth! This does not clash with what we have said, however – for this "concrete faith" is also a human need; man must believe in an absolute and true force, and not just in some kind of "G-dliness within himself." For one cannot speak with himself; to have a relationship, there must be some kind of existence outside oneself, something strong and complete. And therefore we will say that this, too, is part of the faith imbued in man that is so vital for his existence: faith in absolute perfection that is great and external to ourselves.

But once again the question persists: If this, too, is a human need, then how can we know that there is something "really, totally, absolutely true"? The answer is that we cannot be what we are not. A person does not have 100% "pure reason" (as in the title of Kant's work, *The Critique of Pure Reason*). He always has an ulterior motive or need; he always acts according to his individual personality and humanity. Researchers, too, are only human, and not absolute and independent forces, devoid of needs and emotions. This is not a deficiency, but rather exactly how we were created: we are subjective and concerned parties.

It is therefore impossible to seek or contemplate truth that is external to us. We are by definition placed precisely here, in this narrow world with our limited senses: "If I knew Him, I would be Him," wrote R. Yehuda HaLevy in the Book of the Kuzari. Furthermore, a person has no real need to "know Him." Man cannot, and does not want to, be what he is not. Did anyone ever appoint any of us to be an "outside investigator"? According to what we know, sense, and experience – and we have no tools beyond these – the existence of G-d is absolute, and His truth is unequivocal. There is nothing wrong with the fact that I am not objective – for I have no other way, in my lifetime, to judge my surroundings. To force myself to go beyond this is simply compulsive philosophizing and pointless sophistry.

One who has basic, natural faith – what are you lacking? As King Solomon writes, "be happy with your life!" Partake more of the Tree of Life, and less of the Tree of Knowledge!

If Everyone is a Believer, What Then is the Commandment "to Believe"?

What is the point of commanding us to have faith, if we are already automatically there? And what is the point of the Torah's commandments [*mitzvot*] altogether?

The answer is: Since you are created, and you have a Creator Who imbued you with the will to come close to Him and sense His closeness – do it! Shape and strengthen your bonds with Him, and your dialogue with him. The commandment is to make sure you do not deny your own nature, and to flow. Be aware of your power of faith; don't try to outsmart it, but rather let it develop. The *mitzvah* is to live according to your nature, as most of humanity always did until "modern man" came along over the past few hundred years and said, "Let's throw out G-d and coronate Man as our king instead." Modern man thought that if we delve deeper and deeper, and if we work on increasing our abilities to do and make and accomplish, then we'll be able to get along in the world even without faith in G-d and without religion (i.e., our relationship with Him).

But today's modern world is increasingly returning to concepts of subjectivity; man is becoming more humble, less sure of what he knows, less disdainful of the invisible world of the spirit; he is learning more about the strong and interdependent relationship between body and soul, and between physicality and spirituality. He gives more respect to the metaphysical. This is possibly the great innovation of the 20th century: It began with a "big bang" of faith in mankind, of wars and mass murder in the name of all sorts of man-made philosophies to which they related as actual Divinity – but ended with a little whisper of the return to belief in spirit, to forces beyond human, to that which is eternal. And this return, I am confident, has only been gaining momentum since then.

From Faith to the Torah's Commandments

And regarding *mitzvot*: They represent our "acceptance of authority," the framework. Not every *mitzvah* do I understand, yet I still fulfill them all. For if I choose by myself which of them to observe and which not, the truth once again becomes subjective and small; again I'm left with no complete ethical framework; and again I have incomplete G-dliness – which by definition must be complete. I would also be missing "mutuality," i.e., I would again be my own god, with no connection and with no love, with neither a point-of-origin nor destination. If there is faith, there can be love, "in the name of which I gather each morning the small details and little joys of a regular day," as in Rachel Shapira's above-quoted poem. Similarly, even the small details of Jewish Law are performed with joy, because there is for Whom to do so.

I believe that this is what R. Yehuda HaLevi refers to in his above-quoted Sefer HaKuzari: A person can choose whether to believe his father, who heard from his father, who heard from *his* father, etc., that generations ago their father underwent a one-time prophetic experience at Mt. Sinai, together with all the other Jews of that time, in which they received the Ten Commandments, etc. He can also choose not to believe him. The straightforward path in man's thinking is the former: to believe. Yes, one could assume that his father is lying to him, and that *his* father lied to him – but why would he? A normal person wants to live, and not paranoidly cast doubts on everything.

R. HaLevi further explains that while the other religions are built upon a fantastic story that someone once told, the Judaic faith is predicated upon the most basic and natural behavior: a son's belief in what his father taught him and a personal relationship with G-d. Jewish faith is the story of a personal connection with G-d, not scientific theories about His presence. This is healthy psychology, and not dry scientific philosophy.

One of the stories of Rabbe Nachman of Breslov, *The Wise Man and the Simpleton*, tells of a clever man who casts doubt on everything he is told. Until proven otherwise, he believes, all his life is one big uncertainty. And thus he ruined his life... Life is not a courtroom. I once heard from Rav Shagar[35], of saintly blessed memory, that the characters of both the wise man and the simpleton are busily active within man's soul, and that though Rebbe Nachman emphasizes solidarity with the simpleton, he maintains that the wise man's doubts, too, are part of our service of G-d.

And with all this, if a person has so many unanswered questions, it means that the enigma of life is simply becoming more powerful for him. This means that his longing for the secret of eternity, his yearning to encounter something higher than all his questions, his craving to believe in that which cannot be conceived – all this soars ever higher. I once heard from the poet Yonadav Kaploun that when the famous poet Zelda was going through a great crisis of despair

---

[35] The acronym by which Rabbi Shimon Gershon Rosenberg was known - Torah scholar and original thinker, and founder and head of Yeshivat Siach Yitzchak in Efrat

and disappointment, and could not understand G-d – she told him that she then realized that G-d was even greater, even more exalted, and even more incomprehensible than she had realized. Her faith became then even more substantial, spiritual, and sublime.

I see I have gone on at length, and it's now almost Yom Kippur. I wish you a day of great and clear love, with no fear of varying states of soul and spirit.

–Meir

CHAPTER 6

"FORMERLY RELIGIOUS, LONGING FOR LOVE"

July 7, 2011 17:15 GMT

Dear Ayelet,

Sometimes people become religiously observant, or stop being observant, or make other major changes in their lives – and then they can't understand why all their problems haven't all been suddenly resolved! They take an emotional or psychological problem and attribute it to a religious-philosophical matter – because that makes it more manageable and pleasant. But the truth is that one must distinguish carefully between questions of the spirit and questions of the psyche.

You "got messed up," as you put it, with Judaism and belief, and I think the books I recommended to you will help you. But I didn't sufficiently emphasize this point: With all that you've gone through, in an environment that apparently didn't understand you, it would be a good idea for you to work with someone also on raising your self-image.

May you have a Sabbath of peace and serenity, full of love and calm.

Meir

July 8, 2011

Meir,

Thanks very much for your attentiveness and your willingness to help. I really admire all the time that you devote to people...

First of all, I apologize that I'm writing to you on the Sabbath, but that's just how it came out. Forgive me if I'm too open; I have nothing to lose in any event - I really am weak. In my worst dreams I never could have thought that I would feel so alone at age 33. I'm really trying not to sink into despair, and to find strengths from my innermost places. The truth is that it is really not easy...

For example, now it's late Friday night, and I find myself sitting in my apartment, alone, staring at the computer screen, instead of being in a house full of children and a loving husband. I close my eyes, and try to fill myself with strengths that I sometimes just don't know where to draw them from.

I spent this afternoon at a café with a friend, and I acted real strong and as if everything's great – I guess I was saving the tears for the keyboard. I'm so sick of this. I told you that I studied in [such-and-such] Ulpanah [Religious Girls High School] in Jerusalem, which you know is a very demanding place, and I did very well. I could have continued from there along the regular path: a year of volunteer service, college studies, becoming a teacher, getting married, and today I would have been a mother of four or five kids (b'li ayin hara, as you guys would say...), and maybe living in a community in Samaria – a nice, organized, and convenient life. I have friends from the past who live that way today. But this wasn't enough for me; the "other" life seemed more alluring, beautiful, full, varied. The freedom, the creativity – everything called out to me. I'm attractive, so they say, and it gained me lots of good things. Even when I worked as a waitress when I was in college, I knew how to come home after an evening shift with hundreds of shekels. It took me many years to realize that I was on a dead-end road.

I think you're naïve; you don't know what goes on here. I go out with guys, ready to build a home and a family – but they're still far from that, they're in no rush at all. They want to enjoy life to the hilt. They always spoke to us in the Ulpanah and in our youth groups about those who live lives only of "externals" – I didn't understand what they meant; maybe I "fell asleep on the watch," as they say. So now I have everything, and I have nothing. I have a fine career, in charge of 40 workers, and I'm successful. You have to understand, I have a friend my age who says that she has no chance of getting married because she's fat and no one looks at her. She very much wants a child, so she's "ordering" one from the sperm bank. You have to fill out a questionnaire, choose what color eyes, how tall, complexion, all sorts of strange things. Even I, with no religious life at all, pity her and think it's repulsive. But it's not that I'm doing so much better. The relationships that I managed to have, even with deep-thinking guys, ended pretty quickly. I recently decided that for these purposes I'll be "half-religious;" I won't continue on to a physical relationship until we both know that "this is the one." Even if it takes a month, or two months, I don't care. I was going out with someone, actually someone I liked, and after he started dropping hints, I told him of my decision – and he said, "Oh, I thought you were serious." Exactly those words, and he left.

Sometimes I dream that everything was just a bad dream, and that I'm 19 again, innocent and righteous, going to Torah classes, praying, going out with shy Yeshiva boys, weaving youthful dreams like a romantic little girl. I realize that this is not real, and that's not me, but for dreaming... I'm now almost completely cut off from my parents, they're sure that I'm just hedonistic and lustful and nothing else. I caused them great embarrassments, and they repress it. I understand their anger at me, but for myself, I haven't neglected the commandment to "honor your father and mother." If you have a suggestion, I would be happy to hear it. The hope that I originally saw in the "way leading back to my little town" [from a popular song by Yoram Tahar-Lev and Rivka Zohar] has again been lost, and suddenly seems to me totally impractical.

You'll see this letter after Shabbat, so I'll wish you a good week. Thanks, really, for your attention and your help.

Ayelet

Ayelet, Shalom.

What courage!

I'll begin with a personal disclosure: I had feared that perhaps I wasn't sensitive enough in what I wrote to you – so it was a compliment for me to receive such a candid letter from you. I felt it was a vote of confidence.

You know that I live in Jerusalem. There were nights, after my lectures in Tel Aviv, when the long soul-conversations lasted til 2-3 in the morning, and then instead of going home, I would remain for the night in the so-lonely "State of Tel Aviv[36]." But then it would take me an hour or two to fall asleep, because of all the sadness in the world, all the loneliness – too much to even contain. And the word "lonely" itself is

---

[36] a popular reference to the culture and mindset that prevails in Tel Aviv, so different than the rest of the country

so alone, for it never happens that two people talking about loneliness mean the same thing – because then they would not be lonely... I admit there were times that I couldn't take it; I thought I might be getting really burnt out.

You know yourself for 30 years already, while I only know you for a short time. To me, you appear young, successful, vigorous and talented, with all options open before you. As far as I know, you haven't made any irreversible errors in your life (if there is such a thing).

After our talk, while its memory was still fresh, I wrote him an email. To whom? I don't know exactly who he is, but he is the one who is meant for you; I clicked "save." I wrote him that she's a girl with real life-forces, vitality, fire – someone who doesn't fall asleep in life, someone with whom he'll be able to live for almost 90 full years, someone who is electrified and constantly searching. I wrote him that if you're looking for "tea with lemon and the old books" [from a popular song by Arik Einshtein] – she's not for you. But if you want to charge forward and conquer the world, if you're not afraid of risks, or of moods, or of running to start the next mission right after completing the one before it – it would be worth your while to meet her...

Of course, those words are meant mainly for you. If you're always aware of this, you won't enter into relationships that have no chance.

And then your email came. It didn't surprise me at all – because if one is already going through loneliness, it should be experienced all the way; no sense in running away from it. But what I couldn't understand was the despair. You mentioned the "way leading back to my little town," and you said that the longing awakens your dream to go back, to take the path of a "little girl coming home again." We talked once about how it is impossible, by definition, to actually return to innocence. When you described for me how it truly fills you, I felt how strong it was for you, how powerful and genuine. What happened since then? Maybe it's the fear that always comes when something big is about to happen? I would never tell anyone what to do, but given the gist of what you said, it would seem that the solution is to choose only reference points, milestones, things from your old world that still retain a sweet taste.

Society generally takes things superficially. The people around you felt that your questions, your "foolishness," your rebelliousness, were simply your excuse to leave, and that you were just a weak personality encountering small lusts. It's enough that you know that this is not the case; you're already free of the need to appease or mollify any given social sector.

Regarding your parents: I think you should be open with them. This is the genuine "honor of parents," for this is what they want to hear and to know. They want to be involved in your life, including the difficulties. And if it's hard for them to accept you, you'll have to guide them to do so, as much as they can. The main thing is to show them this side of you. Talk to them, or write to them, about the same hardships that you shared with me. Write them that you think their presence in your life will help you. You'll help them get to know a new Ayelet – complex, deep, searching for truth. He, after all, is your father 100% – there's no half-father – and he'll dance for joy all day long just from knowing that his daughter wants him to really listen to her, and believes that he'll do it, and that she's not willing to give up on a relationship that has no substitute. He'll feel that it's just like he would never give up on his relationship with his Father in Heaven, no matter where it takes him – for nothing can take its place. (Just like a little boy who covers his face and asks, "Where am I?" Chabad has many teachings about the Kabbalastic sephira of Keter (Crown), far beyond our Free Will and beyond our understanding – but of course you don't feel like hearing about that...) And your mother will be thrilled to know that you are so close to building a family; that's clear from everything you wrote. Maybe it won't be exactly the type of family that they built, with different emphases and rhythm – but they'll be proud of it.

I have a lot more to add, but the sun is about to set and it's time for me to take a bike ride with my little son before he goes to sleep. To be continued, for sure. I don't think I said anything new, but I hope I managed to help you organize your thoughts a bit.

When I send you a Shabbat Shalom blessing of peace and serenity, I fear that the blessing becomes a curse, so I will just sign off with no blessing...

Meir

CHAPTER 7

ON THE TRANSMISSION OF JEWISH LAW

WHO IS THE POSEK[37]? IS HE OBJECTIVE? IS THERE ANY
FLEXIBILITY IN HALAKHAH? ARE THERE NOT DIFFERENT
INTERPRETATIONS OF A GIVEN VERSE?

...Hello.

This subject has occupied my thoughts for years now, raising many questions for which I have not yet found answers:

The Torah is so rich and intricate, and can be interpreted in many ways. How is it possible to determine that one explanation is better than another? I once decided to do only what is written clearly in the Torah, without any commentary or interpretations; only that whose significance and essence I understand. For instance, "Do not burn fire in all your dwellings on the Sabbath day" (Ex. 35,3) – this is simple and straightforward and undisputed. But then I realized that if I do only what I understand, the power of the concept of "we will do and listen" [signifying blind obedience to G-d's word] is lost.

How do we differentiate between an objective interpretation and one that is essentially an opinion, influenced perhaps by fears, or by the

---

37 This Hebrew term refersr to one who decides matters of Halakhah [Jewish Law]

inability to see more broadly and progressively? Who makes the decisions, and how?

Sincerely,

Meital

Shalom Meital!

Picture this real-life situation: An elderly man lies on his deathbed, attached to an oxygen machine in his home. Hundreds of people come to him every week with their Halakhic queries and problems. He doesn't need books; he has known the Talmud and Halakhic writings by heart since childhood, and has remained sharp throughout his life. As a well-known Jerusalem Halakhic *posek*, he is devoted to answering the questions of people he doesn't know and to whom, ostensibly, he owes nothing.

This basic experience of direct contact with a great Halakhic authority is one that is lacking for most of today's generation. This is my introduction.

The basis of your questions is the disappearing personal component in the transmission of Torah from one generation to the next; this appears to be fading from the horizons of our modern life. This is the main point of my answer.

And now to the issue itself: It is an undisputed historical fact that the secret of the long survival of the Jewish Nation is its one and only Torah, unanimously accepted throughout thousands of years, long exiles, and geographical distances. The differences between various groups and congregations and even philosophies are relatively minor. It would have been impossible to preserve "one Torah" in this manner, under such differing and different conditions of time and place, without a very strong system of authority. This is the reason why the Sages of Israel throughout the generations gave their souls, sometimes quite literally, to preserve and perpetuate the rules of Torah transmission, Halakhic rulings, commentary, and to maintain all the traditions, ethical principles, life secrets, etc. Most people base their views of this system on their short, random encounters with the rich and varied world of Torah creativity – encounters that are often tendentiously edited by the media. In truth, however, the system functions so much more precisely and wondrously than it thus appears.

A. The Critical Need for an Oral Law

The need for an Oral Law based on the Written Law, as the basis for this entire system, is discussed at length in the various Introductions of Maimonides, as well as in his Sefer HaMitzvot (Book of Commandments) and in Nachmanides' critiques thereof. The principle common to these sources is that the Torah itself set the ground rules for its continuity: *"If there arises a matter of judgement too hard for you... You shall go up to the place that G-d will choose... and go up to the judge that shall be in those days... Do according to the ruling and judgement that they shall instruct; do not deviate from that which they tell you right or left"* (Deut. 17,8-11).[38] The Talmud (Tr. Shabbat, p. 23) explains that this verse is the source on which we rely to view the Rabbinic rulings as Divine commands. For instance, we recite "Blessed are You, G-d... Who has commanded us to light Chanukah candles;" although Chanukah is not of Biblical origin and stems rather from the Second Temple era, the Rabbinic injunction to observe Chanukah can be viewed as if G-d commanded us to do so.

The second basis for the Rabbinic network of Jewish Law is the very fact that there is no such thing as a "straightforward reading" of the Torah text. This is because the Torah contains no vowels or punctuation, and our reading of it is enabled only by the traditions handed down through the generations.

Imagine a stagnant system of Halakhah, a frozen Torah, in which the rabbis of the generations had no authority. Would such a system be able to survive? Would it not appear totally detached from our lives, something of another world? The gap between the Torah and people would widen with every generation, and the Torah would become irrelevant to our lives. This would essentially be the death of the Torah.

For instance, let's assume that we had only the Written Torah, precisely as is. It sets out the law

---

[38] Rashi explains, based on the Medrash Sifrei, that this means that even if they tell you that right is left or that left is right, do not deviate from their rulings.

concerning an ox that gored. When was the last time you saw an ox goring someone? Or even an ox altogether? And what would be the law when a dog bites, or if a car runs someone over? Can the car be likened to an arrow that someone shoots, or perhaps to a purposely-set fire that went out of control and caused damage? The Torah does not stipulate these laws; it wants us to extrapolate them. The Torah also commands us to help one whose donkey got stuck along the way – but says nothing about a car stuck along the highway in the middle of the night, requiring just a light push to get it going. One could infer from its lack of mention in the Torah that he might pass it by without offering help. Could this be called a Torah of Kindness?

It is precisely the example you cited – the Sabbath ban on burning fire – that exemplifies the difficulty in understanding the Torah literally and simply. The Karaites, who said they would fulfill only that which is written in the Torah, understand this command to mean that there must be no fire in a Jewish home on the Sabbath – and therefore they forbid eating hot food on the Sabbath. The Sages, on the other hand, were more precise: "Do not burn fire" – but if it is burning before the Sabbath begins, it is permitted[39]. The Karaites said, "You're playing games; we'll just eat cold food." But it's obvious that the entire Torah is written with "codes" and abbreviations. For instance,

---

[39] though they required that it be covered

do the Karaites wear tefillin? How can they know what tefillin are altogether? The Torah says only, "It shall be a sign on your arm and *totafot* between your eyes" – but what does that mean? From the fact that the Torah does not delineate what they look like, it is clear that the Written Torah must be supplemented by orally-transmitted information.

There are Jews who are careful not to smoke on the Sabbath, but have no problem starting up a car. Are they not both a form of lighting fire? Certainly they are, and are both forbidden – but the fire in the car is not seen, and for many people, what they don't see doesn't exist...

I assume that this claifies that there is no way to observe the Written Torah in a systematic, consistent manner without an Oral Torah. The task of the Halakhic *posek* is to derive the definitions in principle from the sources and to implement them in our present-day reality.

B. On the Many Differing Opinions; Objectivity; and Interpretive Democracy

Your next question is: Given that the above is true, how do I choose between the different interpretations? How can I know if there is one that is objective? How can I decide which one is correct?

Well, regarding issues with no practical import that are only matters of interpretation, we say that "there are 70 'faces' [viewpoints] to Torah" and "just as [people's] faces are different, so are their opinions different."

But in matters concerning how to behave according to Jewish Law, there is a very precise system of determining the law, as I mentioned, in which various opinions are raised along the way to a final decision – and the system has been working for many generations. The rules for deciding the Halakhah are clear. There is no one voice that overrides all others; there is a range of opinions and true democracy in expressing them – an extreme democracy, even, with no parallel in any system in the modern world.

As a youth, I once came into a Yeshiva in Jerusalem precisely as the *shiur clali* [general lecture] was starting. Let me here explain that Yeshiva study is generally independent, with only a few classes and lectures. Each student spends most of the day on his own or with a study partner, known as a *havruta*, with whom he reads, clarifies and analyzes the texts, ten or twelve hours a day. Once a day the students, divided usually by age groups, are given a class lesson. And once a week, the Rosh Yeshiva – the Dean – delivers a lecture to the entire Yeshiva. He invests intense work in preparing it, and it then leads to arguments and debates among the students. The Rosh Yeshiva is a venerable scholar, and the students accord him admiration, honor and fear, and "distance."

And so, I found myself in this main lecture, with the Dean standing there and presenting his intricate approach to a particular Talmudic topic. As he was making one of his points, one of the students interrupts and calls out, "Who said so? Why do you understand the source in that way, when perhaps you could explain it in *this* way? etc." The Rosh Yeshiva responds, and then someone else interrupts, and yet another student rushes to bring a book that supports one side or the other. I stand there amazed: What is this *chutzpah*? Who is this cheeky youngster seeking to destroy the lecture, the Rosh Yeshiva's carefully worked-out thesis, before hundreds of students? I'm astonished by this "open market," this free, open and even extreme democracy of ideas. The Dean is "into" it, however, encouraging his students to interrupt, to test things, even to tear down what he has not satisfactorily proven. The truth cannot be shy! There is no partiality; there are arguments, sometimes loud, and perpetual examining of the texts.

One of the greatest Halakhic poskim of the previous generation, Rabbi Shlomo Zalman Auerbach, was invited as a young man to give this type of *shiur clali* as a "test" to see if he could fill the position of Rosh Yeshiva. When he returned home, Rav Auerbach's wife asked him how it went, and he responded sadly that it did not look like he had passed. He explained that someone had asked a question shortly after the lecture began, ostensibly undermining the entire thesis he wished to present. He recounted that he thought for a moment and then said, "That is in fact a very strong question, and it negates my entire approach. I see that I was wrong." He apologized, left the lectern, and walked away.

But in fact, a short time later, the Yeshiva directors officially invited Rav Auerbach to serve as their Rosh Yeshiva. It turned out that his integrity and willingness to acknowledge the truth was more important to them than a mistake that he made – for everyone errs sometimes. They knew that others in his situation might have attempted to dodge the question, or come up with a vague response, or perhaps engage in some hair-splitting *pilpul*, which he certainly had the ability to do. Instead, he acted with purity of spirit – something that is fairly rare in our lives – and they offered him the job. When I look at my rabbis and teachers, some of whom are the leading students of Rav Auerbach, I see this trait as a fundamental principle of their way of life, their study, and their Halakhic rulings.

Just for the sake of comparison, in our democratic political establishment, if the Prime Minister decides that he wants something passed in the Cabinet but he does not have a majority, all he has to do is threaten to fire one or two of his ministers, or hint that they will receive some goodies for voting as he wishes – and this is considered proper democracy. But among Torah sages, when a legal hearing is held, the greatest of them expresses his opinion last – so that the others will not fear to present their own opinions that may differ from his.

C. More on Objectivity, Weaknesses, and Personal Interests

Is there an alternative systematic Halakhic way to interpret the Bible? Have the Reform or Conservative movements come up with a different way to rule on Halakhah? No. They simply nullified large parts of the Torah, and chose for themselves nice ideas and concepts as their way of life. This has nothing to do with Halakhah, or with any legal, binding judicial system. Rather, this is a way of relying on parts of the Bible and Talmud for inspiration, not for law. Reality proves that these movements have no continuation and that their communities abroad are disappearing.

Your questions appear to imply that the Halakhah's method of Torah interpretation is arbitrary. In fact, however, the entire Talmud teaches us that the laws derived by Rabbinic interpretation were handed down as precise tradition from rabbi to student. Moreover, some laws were set by the Prophets – yes, that far back. Today we do not have prophecy, but we do have "sparks of Divine Spirit." It is rare, but you can meet people who can penetratingly "see" through periods of time and through hearts, and whose ways of life and spiritual energies are totally different than those of everyone else we know – to put it lightly. I am not a mystic, nor a "pious fool," but I have experienced in my lifetime meetings with people like this. These are not just legends or stories I heard from others.

Today, as well, there is a large gap between today's image of a Halakhic *posek* as perceived by the average fellow who has never met one, and his actual personality. I can write entire books of anecdotes illustrating their greatness, showing that they are well above everyday politics and sectarianism. I will just give another little example of the rabbi I described above, the head of the Rabbinic Court of the Edah Haredit in Jerusalem. I used to visit him over the years to learn his unique traditions and methods of Halakhic adjudication. Towards the end of his life, he was unable to leave his home, for he was attached to a respirator, without which he could barely breathe. Still he continued to answer his many questioners, day in and day out. Can you even imagine anyone in a parallel legal system taking the time to relate to individuals? In my last meeting with him before his death, he told me how worried he was – not about his deteriorating medical condition, nor about anything of a personal nature. It was rather the security situation of the country at that time that pained him so much. He even outlined for me his predictions on these matters (which, by the way, were quite accurate, though that's not my point).

D. Divine Assistance in Issuing Halakhic Rulings

Another point is that there exists an uncompromising demand upon Halakhic poskim regarding their moral and spiritual level. Constant work on

improving character traits is considered a basic requirement in every Yeshiva. The Torah is not just another science, to be coldly analyzed by an objective
researcher. The Halakhic authority has the position of
one who receives and transmits the Torah from generation to generation, and he does so from a position
of holiness and purity of character.

I will not describe the rabbis with whom I was
close in Yeshivat HaKotel and elsewhere, for I would
not be able to finish... I will just mention a few personalities with whom I was privileged to meet. Rabbi
Simcha Zisel Broide was the head of the Hevron
Yeshiva in Givat Mordechai, Jerusalem. His self-control shone, his every word was calculated, his every movement was purposeful. Rav Dov Eliezrov,
the rabbi of the Jewish prisoners before the War of
Independence, was a man of total sweetness and love
for all. Rabbi Yisrael Zev Gustman, Rabbi Avraham
Cahana Shapira – these are legendary names that I
randomly pluck from my memory, but which probably mean nothing to you. I am not talking about
their illustrious Torah scholarship, but only about the
enormity of their work on character refinement.

Especially when dealing with rulings on practical
Halakhah issues, or when engaging in a judicial Torah
hearing, the posek is granted special Divine providence to ensure that he will not err. In a book by one
of the great poskim of a century ago, Rabbi Yitzchak
Elchanan Spektor, appear some 70 Halakhic responsa

on the topic of agunot, women whose husbands cannot be located. His conclusion in all of them, except for one, was that the woman is free to remarry. He was a man of extreme kindness and compassion, and it can be assumed that whatever we know about him in this area is just a small part of it, for he was totally discrete. There was a case in which a woman's husband had disappeared, and she claimed that he had died several years earlier. Rav Spektor looked carefully into the case and into the relevant sources, and took the unusual step, for him, of forbidding her from remarrying. She could not bear the pain of her loneliness and, knowing his good-heartedness and sentimentality, she held a "sit-down strike" in his waiting room, sitting there for days on end. Every time he would walk out to get a book, he would see her there crying. The Rabbi explained to her that he could not change the Halakhah, and could work only within its framework . He felt his heart breaking every time he passed her. One day, they were all surprised to learn that her husband was actually alive and well in South Africa. A long story, but a classic case of what the Talmud calls "the dead man coming back on his feet." It was then clear to all that Rav Spektor had been Divinely guided and prevented from issuing a false dispensation. (I believe that this is how the early Torah giant Rabbeinu Nissim explained, in his D'rashot HaRan, the prohibition to stray from the Rabbi's ruling 'right or left.')

Every topic and question must be studied and interpreted independently, but the underlying principle that we have outlined here is of utmost importance: Know with whom and with what you are dealing!

- Meir

CHAPTER 8

WHY DOES THE GREAT G-D NEED SUCH SMALL LAWS?

Meir, Shalom.

This might sound a bit argumentative and nit-picking, but though I really do connect with the spirit of Judaism, I can't connect with the small details. What does it matter to G-d whether or not I say a blessing before eating bread? Why does He care if I press a certain button on the Sabbath, or if I put on tefillin or not? The laws even tell you how to get dressed, in what order... Isn't that going a bit far? I love the songs, the prayers, honoring parents, and there are some beautiful *mitzvot* (commandments) – but all these little things...

Doesn't this conservative lifestyle restrict the "flow" of life, and weigh heavily down on creativity and freedom? This Halakhic "regime" builds a framework that freezes and stops the vitality of life. Perhaps without it, we would be more able to access our "inner" selves

–Elad

Dear Elad, Shalom!

I think you have touched precisely upon the problematic aspect of "both sides" – those who are called "religious" and those who are termed "secular."

The Torah should be a "Torah of Life" – not something that negates life or diminishes it. Whenever in history the gap between Torah and "life" became too large, many people left Torah, because they saw it as restrictive and reductive – but they were actually throwing out the baby with the bathwater. As defined so accurately but sadly by Michal (of our group): "Freedom has turned into wantonness, the boundaries have been completely abandoned, and a new trouble has been formed." So now permit me a few words about this issue of "lack of boundaries."

The framework of Halakhah [Jewish Law], in its external structure, appears to be a restrictive system. But in its internal structure, which is less well-known and defined, it is a wondrous Divine system that, when implemented and fulfilled, purifies man's soul so that it can become much more spiritual. The soul will attain the attributes of chessed (kindness), g'vurah (strength, courage), and self-control, all leading to broad Free Choice. The soul will also be filled with good-heartedness, sharpness of thought, sustained ability of emotional self-expression, attention to one's surroundings, and many other traits that refine life.

In addition, the optimistic structure of the soul – that which is accepting, humble, non-judgemental – is the result of the fulfillment of this Halakhic system. This soul structure, as is well-known in all schools of modern psychology, is the primary prerequisite for actualizing the maximum unique potential allotted to each person.

In other words, the Halakhic system is designed to give each part of the body and the soul whatever it needs so that the soul can attain its freedom, leading it to reach its unique self-expression. (We have spoken in past sessions about the different types of souls and their roots).

The problem exists for religious people as well. Fulfillment of the Halakhah sometimes become just technical, as described with the words "a commandment...learned [by rote]" (Isaiah 29,13) – with no thought paid to the "soul" of the Halakhah, to the point where the mitzvah's effect on the soul is lost, if not worse.

Sometimes when I see a "secular" person praying, it appears to me much more authentic, much more of a conversation with G-d, than a prayer of duty to be discharged and checked off. When I see a "secular" woman lighting Sabbath candles, excited at receiving the added soul and spirituality of the Sabbath[40], or however she views it, this is a moment of sanctity.

---

[40] A Holocaust survivor once told me that when speaking with groups about his experiences, he always makes sure to describe at length the special spiritual atmosphere that used to envelope the Jewish neighborhoods in Europe from Friday at sundown until the end of the Sabbath. "You simply could not recognize the working man," he said, "who sweated and toiled all week, as the same man you saw on the Sabbath, with an indescribable Sabbath aura emanating from his entire being."

When I see someone putting on tefillin who was not accustomed to doing so as a child, it has vestiges of the most exalted aspects of this mitzvah. This need not by definition be the case, but people who allow "routine" to wear them down, and do not work on renewal and innovation and deepening their commitment, sometimes find themselves keeping Jewish Law only technically and "for the protocol."

Another problem is one of "mistaken proportions" – too much emphasis on that which is less important, and too little given to the more important. This stems from superficial knowledge of Halakhah. There are also problems that stem from sociological processes and herd behavior, but not from the pure Halakhah.

In summary, my answer is that the problem of the gap between the "great G-d" and the small Halakhic details is truly liable to exist – but only when the Halakhah is observed incorrectly. But when the Halakhic framework is utilized properly, the person will become more flexible and "flowing" in his life, enabling him to fulfill his unique destiny.

Incidentally, I generally hear this question from people who find it hard to commit to *any* type of details in their lives, and not just to the details of Halakhah. I first encountered this phenomenon in its extreme form when I began working in Tel Aviv, and I was taken totally by surprise. I met people so en-slaved to the concept of "freedom" that they aren't even free to commit to something they really want, all because "commitment" negates "freedom." This actually led me to write a poem, which I include here below. I showed it to a friend who is a top violinist, a teacher of violin in north Tel Aviv, mainly to children of prominent figures, the "cream of the crop." He told me that he has students who, already in the very first lesson, actually argue with him about how to hold the bow and violin. "No, I would rather hold it backwards," the little son of a well-known Knesset Member tells him. "It's more comfortable for me that way. It's my decision, this is a democracy." And I'm not even talking here about the teacher's lowered status in the eyes of the child, who feels so free to argue with him, since after all he's the teacher's "employer." Here are some more slogans of this "religion of freedom:"

Want to let love die? Get married!

Want to choke your child's creativity and independent thought? Send him to school!

Want to earn money? Quit your job and become self-employed!

I know many followers of this religion who have reached an age and situation from which there's no turning back, and they now greatly regret adhering to this "faith" during the critical years of their lives.

Have a great summer, and regards to Ziv. (Ask him to tell you about the Hassidut of Karlin and its

melodies; they really have an "extra soul" there[41].)
–Meir

TEL AVIV, NEAR JAFFA
by Meir Dorfman
(a free translation from the original Hebrew)

Going down to the sea, towards Tarshish[42],
Fleeing to the Tarshish religion,
To the new, stormy religion
Just like the sea and the waves, like the movie.
Tarshish-style, she takes care to be unkempt,
streaming wherever the wind takes her...
Making sure not to commit
To you or to anyone else.
She loves her "I", and "I"
Talks about "I" to "I"
She takes a dip in the sea, or sinks into wine.
She thinks she still might have a father,
But a mother she most certainly has: the street café.
Addicted to freedom, to the stimulating, to the beautiful.
Very devoted to the commandments,
not free to miss
Even a trivial custom of the heavy freedom
In which nothing may be repeated twice
And in which that which is wonderful today,
Doesn't exist tomorrow.

---

[41] "Extra soul" is a term that stands for greater-than-usual spiritual heights. The Talmud states that we are provided with an "extra soul" on the Sabbath.
[42] as the Prophet Jonah did when he sought to avoid fulfilling his Divine mission

She doesn't promise, she doesn't connect
She doesn't decide – just contemplates,
"OK, just today!" But then, "maybe tomorrow as well?"
She feels she is never late,
She volunteers for everything – but never commits,
Never sure if she hates or loves.
True, as an artist, she "feels like" having a stage
But as one who is free, she will appear only without
preparation.
She is against cooking, but in favor of eating;
Against learning, but in favor of knowing all!

A RELATED QUESTION FROM A DIFFERENT STUDENT:

Hi Meir,

Lately the talk in the media is about the Rabbinate and Halakhic rulings by different rabbis. It really infuriates me. I cannot accept an institutionalized authority that tells people what they cannot eat, what they cannot wear, and whether public transportation is permitted on the Sabbath. And the differences that they enacted between men and women also infuriate me. The issue of women covering their hair and dressing modestly is also very strange to me; I think that real modesty is in one's heart. I tried a few times to talk about it with rabbis after their classes; they didn't look at me directly, but only said, "Speak to my wife, she'll help you." In my opinion, this is really a badge of shame for the rabbinical establishment - seeing a person according to gender. In short, all these little detailed laws just distance me from Judaism – even though I actually see much beauty in the concepts of Judaism. I know that you do not represent those rabbis, but I'm sure you have an opinion on these matters. Thank you.

--Shelly (the redhead from the Wednesday class)

Shalom Shelly,

I totally identify with the sharp tone of your questions. I also identify with your complaints against the detailed collection of laws and prohibitions. You are right that this feeling causes distancing, and leaves little room in the soul for fulfilling mitzvot altogether. But still, when I read between your lines I see - forgive me - much ignorance, which is not your fault. It is caused by the superficial manner in which most Jews of our generation encounter Judaism - usually on the level of sensationalist journalism. I grew up with a totally different Judaism, one in which there is much love, compassion, wisdom, and humanity.

These "authorities" that you view negatively, the true men of Halakhah, appear in the typical secular conception to be ignorant, insensitive, dark, domineering, misogynistic, and sometimes ruthlessly

ambitious and greedy. But having studied Torah under them for many years, I know them not from the
TV screen. I actually see them as the "men who hud-
dle in their coats in the rain... who, if they only could,
would give their lives to save you from poverty or
sickness[43]." Thus, we have different points of depar-
ture – and when setting out to meet the Halakhah,
this makes all the difference. You sound like you
feel threatened by Halakhah– but if so, you've tak-
en a wrong turn along your way. You've come to the
wrong address; Jewish Law is not there at all, and
certainly it cannot be that that's where G-d is. For He
created the world for the benefit of those He created,
to uplift them, and surely not to repress any of the
very strengths and talents that He Himself implanted
within them.

Among the examples you mentioned, allow me to
relate to the one where I feel more on your side, and
in fact where the Halakhah generally supports you:
a rabbi who sends you to his wife. Perhaps we can
look at this from a different place? After all, he grew
up in a different atmosphere – one he did not choose
– and he feels that it is more modest for you to speak
with his wife. Why view this as if he is coming out
with hurtful declarations? One might disagree with
this conservative lifestyle, but why think that it stems
from something bad? It appears strange to you, for

---

[43] Based on a popular song by Rachel Shapira and Nachum Heiman, referring to those
who prefer to avoid the limelight but remain loyal and act kindly even towards those
who ignore them

sure, because you grew up in a different society. There are aspects to this issue of modesty that are connected to social mores , or to what we are accustomed to, and there are aspects that depend simply upon each individual. Let's choose to look at it from a place of respect, with broad-mindedness and inclusiveness. Why should we feel threatened by it?

And who said that this modesty comes at the expense of love and appreciation? (I'm not talking about what happened in those specific incidents, I'm rather talking in general.) I admire people who act like that rabbi more than I do those "extremists" in the opposite direction, those many men who take advantage of their authority to treat women abusively. We all saw that type of thing when we were in the army, in the way many officers treated their female clerks, or the way reservists talked to their female instructors. Why should young women have to suffer such treatment? (Not to mention the deterioration that has occurred over the last few years in this regard and the trend to mix the sexes in parts of the regular army, as is well-known.)

The late Rav Shlomo Zalman Auerbach was one of the greatest Halakhic authorities of our generation, whose lifestyle was hareidi in every sense. He was a Rosh Yeshiva in the Bayit Vegan neighborhood of Jerusalem, and insisted on taking a bus every day to the Yeshiva from Rechavia, up until he reached old age. I heard a story about him, which I can't say is true with certainty, but it is characteristic of him. One day, a student of his saw him sitting on the bus, and noted that he remained there past his stop, only getting off one stop later - from where he walked back. The student was curious, perhaps wanting to learn from his behavior, so he asked him for an explanation. The rabbi said: "At the stop before mine, a woman got on and sat down next to me. I figured that if I would get up from my seat right then to get off the bus, she would think I was getting up in order not to sit next to her because she was a woman, and perhaps she would be insulted. So I remained sitting for an extra stop."

Three hundred thousand people were at this man's funeral, which closed up all of Jerusalem – yet barely any "secular" journalist ever heard of him before his death...

The Halakhah is replete with many debates about what takes priority over what, and how to behave when the needs of life appear to conflict with the Torah's demands. For me, it is actually calming to know that there are great Halakhic authorities in the world, because their capacity to rule leniently grows as they themselves grow in Torah learning and in their own character.

Regarding the details of Halakhah I will write separately; there is so much to say about this. But what is critical in my opinion is actually not the details, but our approach to them. The Book of Proverbs states,

"Do not denigrate your mother when she has grown old" – we must approach our ancient traditions with modesty.

With great blessing,

Meir

CHAPTER 9

TIRED OF LOOKING FOR MY DESTINY

Shalom Kfir!

Between the lines of your recent emails, I detect a measure of tiredness – that you've gone through a lot and have tried many different paths, and how exhausting it is to try yet again with openness and enthusiasm. So why don't you just give up and take a different path? – Because you are determined that this is your destiny, your mission.

The truth is that when you wrote about your fear that you might go through your whole life without attaining your destiny, I felt more confident for you. I have a friend who says that in life, you have to do that which you're afraid of. When he finds himself at a crossroad in life, he checks himself to see which is the hardest path, and that's the one he chooses - because that's apparently the true and right one for him. The idea is that if it wasn't right for you, it wouldn't arouse within you such an emotional reaction, to the point of fear. So what is it then? It is that the challenge is great and awakens great fears – not only of failure; even of success.

I would like to tell you something that happened to me – similar in form to what happened to you, but totally different in content. I spent many years seeking out a rabbi and teacher who could teach me in a very specific style. I was full of criticism, and I knew exactly what I was looking for. This was an all-encompassing need that really blocked my creativity and stopped me from writing. I trekked throughout the country to find what I was looking for, and I met some fascinating Torah sages, the oldest of whom are no longer with us. The trips provided a great and rare experience in and of themselves – maybe I'll write about those special meetings one day – but I came up empty-handed. I totally gave up.

Right around then I received a call-up for reserve duty, precisely at the right time for me and exactly what I needed: a "vacation" of guard duty on the pastoral shores of the Dead Sea. Just then, on the heels of my despair, I had a dream about someone specific, someone I didn't know. The dream included exact details, including a strange name I had never heard before. I didn't pay much attention, and only when I got home from the army did I get around to telling my wife. She got all excited, and said that dreams have meaning, and that I should try to find this man. Not very enthusiastically, I looked for and found the name in the phone book, but I didn't know what to do with it, so I did nothing.

After a while, I met in Tel Aviv with Rabbi Mordechai Auerbach, son of the late renowned Rav Shlomo Zalman Auerbach. He told me, "Stop searching - there's no such thing!" He said that there are two types of people: "those who create, and those who test things; it's a question of character and personality, not necessarily a stage in life. Of course there is such as thing as a rabbi/teacher passing the tradition on to his student - but this structure that you're looking for, whereby you so strongly cancel out yourself, is not correct." He also said: "You don't have to always come as a student, thus blocking your own creativity. If you have creativity of your own, and innovative thinking – who are you afraid of? Believe in it, publish your own book, and don't be afraid to teach others."

He then asked me: "Who do you think was my father's rabbi?" I answered what I knew, and he did not deny it, but rather said, "The main aspects of his Torah path that people know today - he did not learn from his teachers, but rather formulated on his own." Until then I had never heard such a clear statement to this effect, and never even considered taking such a direction. He opened a door for me, and in fact I published a book of my original thoughts, and I began teaching in several places.

And then, at the end of our talk, he mentioned off-the-cuff that he knew of a rabbi who could suit me, someone who delves into issues the way I had described. He gave me a letter, asked me not to open it, and told me to deliver it to a certain address. I remembered my dream, and it was the same address and the same person! I phoned him, made an appointment, and arrived at his home with the clear sensation - even before I met him - that I had found what I was looking for. This was many years ago. He lives in Meah She'arim – the last place that I would have gone to look for my ideal teacher. Even now I still go to learn with him whenever the opportunity arises. I have barely ever told this story to anyone, not even to that rabbi, and I also never found out what was written in that letter.

Why am I telling you this? Because I have a feeling that you can learn something from it regarding your own situation, in terms of going with your intuition and listening to yourself more. Think about it.

With deep admiration and great affection,
Wishing you much peace and tranquility,
Meir

August 23, 2009 12:53

Hi Meir,

Thank you for the story you wrote me. I am not sure I totally understood your intention, but it opened the way for me to have "encouraging, strengthening thoughts."

Maybe your friend is right. In a talk we once had, you asked me to define a little more clearly what it is I'm looking for. The truth is, I don't have a definition for this search, because it keeps changing, and then I feel that what I wanted a few months earlier, what I dreamt about and fought for, no longer interests me. How can this be? How do you explain it?

The rhythm of my life has totally changed ever since I moved here. Strangest of all is just being in Jerusalem. They say that Tel Aviv is a country in itself – and I think that Jerusalem is totally a nature reserve. Everything here is so impossibly different: the people, the scenery, the discussions, the dress, the fabric. It seems that the more years pass over this city, the deeper the slumber it falls into, like the final hours of the night. I'm sure I'll get used to it, and meanwhile it's very nice and even magical. What in Tel Aviv is considered eccentric, here is considered mainstream.

Have a good week, and thanks for listening, sharing, and answering. I'm sending you some poems that I wrote – nothing special, but you asked.

Kfir

Shalom Kfir!

How beautifully you write! I read the poems you sent, and I'll write you my thoughts about them in a separate email. It whetted my appetite to read more of your compositions. (I'm sure there must be more - and if not, what are you waiting for?!) If there are others ready to be shown, I would love you to send them.

You wrote about Jerusalem, so I'll also write a bit about my feelings towards this city that I have lived in since I was a child. Every time they tear down an old building, or dig up one of the wadis, or mar the skyline, even if it's to build a road or a new building or luxury project – I feel that I have been wounded. But the more they wound this city, or cut into its flesh, or do whatever they do – it remains beautiful and innocent and virgin. No one can truly harm its beauty.

Maybe I wasn't clear enough about the story I wrote last time, so I'd like to explain it better. Many times we reach a state of spiritual and mental fatigue, and we interpret it as weakness or burnout. And that's true, but it's a mechanism that is a "call for life." The proof is that so many times we find what we are seeking only after we give up. What this means, I believe, is that when we're about to give up, it's time to "upgrade the dream." The old dream, and its enthusiasm, has reached its expiration date, and the soul now requires greater depth and profundity. This doesn't mean that the former dream had no value, but only that it's no longer relevant for us.

And since, as is known, a good question is already half the answer, in the essence of the precise definition of the search is hidden your own creativity.

The "mediator" rabbi in essence opened for me the possibility of telling myself: "Maybe, after all, it's not the right thing to go looking for everything by others and to cancel out yourself before them. It might be causing you to lose your attention the voice that has been granted you."

Kfir, try to read – and apply to yourself – the blunt words of R. Nachman of Breslov about himself, which went something like this: "I have won and I will win; I finished, and I will finish; I am a river that purifies all stains. I am a man of wonder, and my soul is a great wonder; I am something new that the world has never encountered before."

He was humble in understanding that G-d gave him his great abilities - and not so that he should keep them for himself. He understood that he wasn't born to deny his abilities or to choke off the creativity within him. Furthermore, R. Nachman wanted *everyone* to feel this way vis-à-vis his own uniqueness and his mission.

The idea of the changing dreams and your changing search in their wake brought me to put together a class that I gave about two weeks ago on the topic of "Losing and Finding." It focused on the existential paradox of man, who always finds what he isn't looking for and doesn't find what he is looking for. (As is known, there are those who go out to look for donkeys and find royalty instead[44], but there are even more people who search for royalty and don't even find donkeys. Why? Because the search must focus on "What did I lose?" and not on "What will I find?"

---

[44] a reference to the King Saul (based on Samuel I 9), who set out to find his father's lost donkeys but ended up being anointed as King of Israel

It must not center around looking for "finds" (the lost objects of other people), but looking for my own lost objects. We must look inward rather than outward. Then, when we do not find, it probably means that in the hidden recesses of our heart, we are looking for something new, something that we did not lose, something that doesn't really belong to us.

Thank you, and may God bless you and your creative energies.

   - Meir

CHAPTER 10

HOW WILL I RECOGNIZE MY SOUL MATE?
ON TWIN SOULS, MY OTHER HALF, AND FINDING MY DESTINED SPOUSE

Wednesday, Aug. 26, 2009 1:07 AM

Shalom Meir,

I've been attending your classes for a few months now. I don't usually speak up to express myself, even though I sometimes have ideas on how to explain the sources that you cite. I have a tremendous thirst for spiritual nourishment. Ever since I discovered HaMakom [The Place], I feel that I really *have* found my place, one that is spiritual and without pressure. I sometimes come in tired and a bit sad, and leave happy and full, calm and serene.

I would like to share with you a very personal difficulty in my life; maybe you could help me with some advice. Its spiritual dimension is more important to me than the issue itself, how to understand it in terms of religion and faith. It's true that I do not observe the mitzvot, but I have great faith. A few years before I met my husband Itamar, I went out with another guy for six years (!). It was intense; he was my first love, and I thought we would get married. In the end it didn't happen, and we broke up. I later met

Itamar, and within a year and two months we were married. This was a relatively short period to get to know each other before such a fateful decision. He is a very knowledgeable man, a lecturer in physics, his students like him a lot, he's industrious and has many good qualities. We live together serenely, married almost three years, and we lack for nothing. But that other guy remains the mythological "ex", and I live with the constant feeling that he was actually my true intended life partner. With Itamar, I have a settled and steady relationship – but no sparks. We have very very different personalities, hobbies, fields of interest, opinions, outlooks, and personal taste – and this reduces our relationship to a technical level of who's buying what, who fixes the car, etc. Our emotional ties are on a very basic level: "How was your day today?" and the like. So this is my personal confession.

Do you have any kind of explanation regarding whether it's possible to "miss" your intended life partner? And if so, then what does it mean to be married to someone other than your intended spouse? It's not that this has any practical implications for me, but I think that if I would know how it works, I would feel calmer.

See you on Wednesday,

Sincerely,

Avigayil

Shalom Avigayil!

I was greatly moved both by the background of your story and by your openness. I have many thoughts about what you wrote, but I'm a bit too pressured to put them on paper right now. I am very curious to know in what creative areas you engage – because it's obvious from the way you write and express yourself that there are such.

I'm happy that you find a kind of "spiritual home" in HaMakom. Do you ever read the poems of Zelda? There's something there reminiscent of your "accepting" approach to life, even in those areas that are most important to us. I'll write more later, but for now I just wanted to make one comment that occurred to me immediately upon reading what you wrote: A year and two months is a very long time to get to know someone. I would think that even two months are enough. We humans are all made from the same mold, albeit a complex one. Give yourself credit that for such a long period, you were very aware, and could not have fallen asleep on the watch; even if you couldn't fully absorb or define every aspect of his personality, you certainly came to know him as a whole. You have to think about that period and understand it, as well as the fundamental points where his personality and yours intersected. This is difficult work, but it is predicated on the basic faith that things are guided from above – and this allows you not to have to worry about whether you made a mistake.

A fine and good-hearted person, as you described your husband Itamar, is not something to be taken for granted these days. As I said, I will elaborate later.
  –Meir

Shalom Meir,

Thank you for relating to what I wrote. I personally feel as if the year and two months were a short moment, perhaps in comparison to the six years before that. In answer to your question, you were right: I am a writer, of both journalism and prose; I have a newspaper column... I also read a lot. I never heard of Zelda's poems; what, when? I'll have to look on the internet.
I appreciate the time you give me. Thank you very much.
  –Avigayil

Dear Avigayil,

This is a letter I wanted to write leisurely, at length, as appropriate to a heavy topic like this. The Rebbe of Kotzk[45] once said that the decision whom to marry is the most important decision in our lives, and should therefore require at least 80 years of life experience – and yet of all decisions, it's precisely the one that is

---

[45] Rabbi Menachem Mendel Morgenstern, among the greatest thinkers of the Hassidic movement, author of a sharp and cutting philosophy.

given to young people... This says something about what our natural attitude towards marital bonds should be.

The topic you raised is a fascinating one. Some years ago I was a lecturer in Shuva Institute, for girls who are just before, after, or during army or national service, from religious and non-religious homes. They would often ask me about the great difficulties involved in deciding on a partner for life: "How are we to know about the 'sources of souls,' and who is our 'twin soul,' our 'other half' and the like? Could it be that a person would make a mistake and live his entire life in error? Is it possible that a person might not meet the one who, our Sages teach, was intended for him or her 40 days before conception? What happens when people get divorced? And what happens when a widow or widower remarries – who truly is his or her complementary 'soul-mate?'" From where was I supposed to bring them answers? Perhaps the Kabbalists have answers, but the main message I had for them was that there are many layers in Judaism. There is Kabbalah, Halakhah, inner aspects and externals, various approaches – and there are priorities. Who ever said that a Jewish outlook must include the Kabbalistic/prophetic calculations of "sources of souls"?

And so, after this introduction, I would like to add some other ways of looking at and dealing with these questions.

1. You wrote that you believe in G-d. When a person believes, he feels a basic security that he is in "good hands." This removes from your shoulders all responsibility for the results (after the fact, of course). My brother of blessed memory died nearly a year ago. He had a terminal illness, and was perfectly conscious of his situation. I once asked him: "When you're in your hardest moments, suffering terribly, alone – how do you deal with it? How do you get strength? What do you tell yourself?" He answered me: "I remind myself over and over that I am in good hands. I do the best I can, I do what is right – and G-d will give me precisely the amount of years and days that He sees fit."

The faith that "I am in good hands" also tells us that personal Divine providence exists for every single person[46]. Everything that a person does, even if it appears to him that he is initiating and choosing, is actually from and of God. In a book on marriage by Rav Arush[47], he repeats numerous times the idea that the foundation of success in married life is the belief that one's spouse is precisely the one that was designated for you, and that he or she is the absolute best one for you, and that even if you don't understand why, God sent you the person who is best for you. Given this principle, our work on making our marriage great becomes easier and more effective. There's

[46] Perhaps only on condition that he wants it, according to the Rambam.
[47] A leading contemporary Breslov rabbi and teacher.

nowhere to run, we have to work inward. There are no doubts constantly arising to distract from and impede our marriage efforts. We can say that this faith obviates the need to wonder all our lives whether we made the right decision. Instead, our energies regarding the marriage can all be directed to strengthening the bonds, rather than to the doubts that each one might have regarding the other, which are the most "un-marriage-like" thing that can possibly be. A husband and wife who believe that they are truly meant for each other invest most of their marriage vigor in "How?" and not "If." They can talk about every problem without the constant threat that the bonds might fall apart. This brings them to a higher level of will and responsibility, for they are investing in their mutually secure future.

2. Even a "soul that was cut in half" – who says it was divided into identical parts and not different parts? And who ever said that every aspect of our lives must be shared by our spouse? Of course there is no relationship that can come close to the bonds of a husband-and-wife, but at the same time, we can certainly have very close friends for a favorite activity, or for heart-to-heart talks, or at work, or for study and for subjects of mutual interest – or even for hobbies such as mountain-climbing, skiing, or scuba diving, or for a creative arts experience in which our spouse has no interest and cannot share with us. The thought that my spouse can fill in for everything that I lack is a

type of escapism, and a search for someone to blame for my own faults.

What happened during that year and two months? What did you see in him? The answer is that you saw in him that which was important to you but in which you were lacking. This is simple and basic psychology that you can read in all the books.

3. And something else from Hassidut: R. Nachman of Breslov often emphasizes the concept of "internal contradictions in the soul and spirit," and he says that even if they remain unresolved, that's OK, since that's how the soul is. Not only was he not afraid of complexities, but he actually made an ideology out of them (to the point that a contemporary psychologist once wrote that he had "analyzed" the psyche of R. Nachman and reached the conclusion that he was schizophrenic...). Regarding soul-mates and zivug[48], R. Nachman wrote that there are many different levels and aspects thereof, even if many of them have no practical application. For instance, he wrote, if a couple married and later divorced, it means that in some way or another, this was the relationship that was supposed to have been formed, and that up to the time of the divorce, the designated higher-spiritual aspects did actually come to pass. But more than that: Even if they never married, but were only engaged, this too is a certain level of intended soul-partnership, and was not for naught; the engagement completed

---

[48] Literally, "coupling" or "union, and often referring to one's pre-destined match.

the "upper partnership" of their souls. And even if they only thought about getting engaged, and even if they only met and then decided not to continue the relationship, and even if they only planned to meet but didn't actually do so, this also has an element of the ultimate partnership. And even this: If someone is just sitting at home and says to his friend, "Hey, what do you think about setting up such-and-such with so-and-so?" and then the other answers, "What?! They have nothing in common!"- this, too, is the implementation of some aspect of soul-mating that according to G-d's plan was supposed to be in the world[49].

It's true that in our generations, we don't have too many people who understand these things. Sometimes the rule is: "He who knows doesn't say, and he who says, doesn't know" (as the Chazon Ish[50] said once about those who like to "predict" when the Redemption will come).

This is a very broad topic, and I wrote only some starting points from which to begin thinking about it.

Even though you wrote that your questions are just so you can understand and not for practical application, I would still like to recommend that you work on it. I don't know if the two of you talk openly about

---

[49] According to the Kabbalah, human souls were created in pairs. When they descended to the world, they separated, and some of our work in this world is to reconnect them and rectify the separation. The novel idea to which R. Nachman is referring is that this rectification or completion is actually complex, because every soul has a different need in this completion process. And because there are different levels of completion and rectification, there are also different levels of actualization in these relationships.

[50] Rabbi Avraham Yeshayahu Karelitz of Bnei Brak, Israel. One of the leading Torah giants of the last century, he is known by the name of the works he wrote.

this difficulty, about the dryness that you feel. I think that there is so much that can be done, either alone or with the help of marriage counseling. Your lives could be so much sweeter! It would really be worth it. Good night. I hope I didn't tire you out too much.
    -Meir

                Monday, August 31, 2009 12:40 AM
Thanks very much for your detailed answer. You didn't tire me at all; on the contrary. You planted new thoughts that deepen my view of the situation, but also raise new questions. But I still don't understand what your answer is to my question as to whether it's possible for a person to live his entire life having missed his "twin soul?"
    –Avigayil

Avigayil, Shalom.

I don't know the answer – but as they say in the Yeshivot, *mai nakfa mina?* What's the practical significance of this question? What functional ramifications does it have? It's better just to assume that there is no possibility of missing your meeting with your twin-soul mate. And if it looks like there was a miss, that means that this is precisely how your intended soul partnership was Divinely supposed to unfold.

I'll tell you an amazing story, which until it

happened, I never believed could happen except in fairy tales. I knew a bachelor, 59 years old, a very fine man who never married and lived alone. I cringed a bit every time I met him. One time I had a chance to have a nice open talk with him, and he poured his heart out. He said he'd had many relationships, but they were never able to really take off – and he knew why. There was a girl his age whose life paralleled his in many ways, and they had crossed paths at many different junctures, ever since childhood. It began in elementary school, continued in high school, then they met by "chance" in the army several times, and then again in college. She was always the "queen of the class," he said, the most successful, the prettiest, the smartest, always full of life and confidence – and he knew he had no chance to win her. This childish analysis and image remained with him for years, even after he grew up and understood that it was not to be. But deep in his heart he always kept an imaginary hope, like an impossible dream, that sweetened his life. He always remembered what was sort of the "final straw." One day, when he was still in university, it was his turn to give a lecture before other students on papers they had written. Coincidentally, one of the students in the audience was this woman. Throughout the lecture he saw on her face a look of disdain and condescension – reawakening the old pain in his heart. And then suddenly she got up and left, as if to say, "What nonsense! Who has the patience to hear this?!" She didn't say it, of course, but her body language was clear – as were her silences, he later told me. That was the knock-out for him, the end of the sweet dream. He had other relationships afterwards, but somewhere deep inside, she always remained, with her image clouding over every romantic association he would form.

When he told me this, I was sure I had heard a similar story before, but I simply could not figure out who or when. It continued to bother me, until one day the mystery was solved. It turns out that my wife had had a very personal talk with a woman in a weekly class she used to go to, and the woman told her about a man she had been head over heels in love with ever since childhood. She said she always tried to get his attention, but he kept on rejecting her. She waited for him at a thousand different junctures, and he always pointedly ignored her, and certainly never initiated anything or gave her a chance. She said that the breaking point came when she happened to hear him give a lecture… She sat and listened, barely paying attention, just looking and thinking about him the whole time – until finally she felt a choking in her throat, and was about to burst into tears. So, to save herself, and him, from the embarrassment, she quickly got up and left. She can't get him out of her head, she said, maybe she was never the right one for him, etc. etc.

The end of the story is complex – they ended up

reuniting, without bitterness or second-guessing over what they had lost – but my point is different. This is clearly a heart-wrenching story: A man and woman 59 years old, both of them with very high emotional awareness (she treats people for emotional issues), and yet in their personal lives acted like little children for so many years – as if everything got stuck back when they were kids. Was this sad miss inevitable? Maybe they flubbed a chance to bring new life into the world; who can ever know? But at least they didn't wallow in regrets. They believed that this was the destined path, and their joy in their reunion was greater than their sadness at what had gone wrong. They realized that being stuck in the past would not benefit them, but rather the opposite.

And so, I think you should ask yourself: What now? What's next, and how? What is the maximum benefit that can result from this for our marriage? These are the correct, constructive questions, and not those that we cannot answer, such as "What if?" As you know, our prophets have not yet returned…

With great faith and wishes for your great success,

–Meir

CHAPTER 11

WHY SO MANY SABBATH RESTRICTIONS?

"The thing about Shabbat that makes it so hard for me is that there seems to be no real connection between what the Torah says about Shabbat, and the Shabbat laws that we observe today!

"In addition, it used to be that lighting a fire was very difficult – getting flint and rubbing stones together until they caught fire – whereas today it takes just a second. I can understand that we shouldn't work hard in the fields, or in construction, and the like, and that a day of rest is needed – but what's wrong with drawing a picture, for instance? For me, drawing gives me life, and when I'm in the countryside on Shabbat, I see the beautiful horizon and I just draw; it gives me inspiration. I totally enjoy it, and certainly don't feel like I'm 'working'..."

The Torah source that defines forbidden Sabbath work activities is the proximity of two passages: the description of the creative work involved in building the Mishkan (Tabernacle), and the ban on work on the Sabbath. Just as in every text, the Torah has rules of editing, and they are called the "Measures [Rules] by Which the Torah is Interpreted." Among these rules is the order and placement of laws in the Torah.

The Mishkan was essentially a temporary Beit Mikdash, designed to embody all the basic life elements. In the Beit HaMikdash are manifest, in their essence, all human strengths – the various forces of mind and spirit, the different forms of intellect and wisdom, and all the senses. The process of building the Mishkan encompasses the whole spectrum of human creativity and achievement. This is what is known as melacha, forbidden Sabbath work.

In my opinion, the root of this word is the same as the word for "emissary" – malach (angel), indicating that the spiritual potential is connected to its actualization via action.)This is true not only in Hebrew, but also in English: "emissary" and "mission," referring to "action," also appear to be from the same root.) That is, the action is a mission that connects between that which is unprocessed, the potential, and its objective – the final developed product. Forbidden Sabbath work is that which is defined as a creative act; it is not the work per se that is prohibited, but rather the creation. The definition of such work is therefore not related to the toil that is invested, but rather to the wisdom involved in effecting a change from one state to another. The Creator wants us to remember that together with all our strengths and abilities, we are not eternal; we are not "creators," but "created." One day a week we immobilize our "creative" abilities in the world, all of our accomplishing and doing, and return to the passive facets of our personalities. Sabbath is a day devoted to the spiritual part of our soul, which pays humble attention to the voices of Creation.

Sabbath is the day on which we take a low profile, and minimize all types of making and fashioning. We direct everything inward, not outward, and we sense man as having been "created," a gentle reflection of perfection, as if he is "a part of G-d above[51]." One day a week we are as if in the World to Come, the complete world that no longer needs to be completed or repaired. Acts of creation generally come to rectify or fill a certain lack, but here we have an entire day on which nothing needs to be created; we simply gaze with contentment at all that has been created.

When I once released a series of CD's of my cantorial performances, I was at first, characteristically, quite self-critical, and though they were selling well, I didn't listen to them for some three years. But then I listened, and they were great! I couldn't even remember what faults I had found. Similarly, on the Sabbath, we are like an artist taking stock of his works from a wider perspective, without criticism.

I once heard a great description of this state of "lowered profile." I was serving as a cantor in South Africa, with an accompanying choir. I'm not sure how observant the members were, but the policy of

---

[51] Baal HaTanya, based on Job 31,2

the local Rabbinical court was to "bring everyone in" as much as possible, and not to rebuff anyone. (This was a policy that proved itself.) In any event, I once overheard a very non-Halakhic chat between two members, in which one said, "You can't imagine what keeping the Sabbath is like. I started doing it recently. The most wondrous moment is when Shabbat comes in. The feeling is just out of this world. All at once it becomes totally quiet and calm. No phones, no TV, no radio, no computer, no internet, no noise of washing machines or cars or food processors. Serenity just comes upon you." The other member, with a dreamy look, responds, "Wow, I wish I could keep the Sabbath too!" So the first one says, "What's the problem? Why can't you?" "Because I live far from the synagogue..." "So move closer to the synagogue, just like I did, and then you can keep the Sabbath!"

CHAPTER 12

ON SEPARATION AND DIVORCE

Hi Shmulik –

I've been thinking a lot about what you told me yesterday, the direction the two of you are taking towards separation. It's very sad for me, regardless of whether it is right or not; you know how dear you are to me. And it is even sadder after I had a deep talk with Atarah and… I don't get it. She herself sounded surprised. I know that I don't really know anything, and I don't profess to be able to intervene, but my heart tells me: Despite all, maybe something can change? Perhaps it's not final? Maybe it's just a bad dream?

On the way home, I told myself: "Remember proportions. Maybe in Tel Aviv this is how it is, like changing jobs." But then as I tried to sleep at night, it just wouldn't let me go. I began to think: "Why, really, did they choose to tell me? Maybe they wanted to see my reaction." I obviously don't know what's going on between you, but I have to say that from what I heard last night, my personal feeling is that a careful decision was not made here, and that not enough effort was made to fix and overcome difficulties. I am not one to criticize; I don't do that. But this pain at the finger so quick on the trigger of divorce, the frivolous ease with which such a decision is made, the seeming rashness, causes me to depart from my usual practice. Of course there are cases when divorce is the right choice, but even then our Sages use extreme imagery to describe it: "One who divorces his first wife, even the Altar sheds tears for him." That is, it is so sad that even unfeeling rocks feel it. To whom are these words addressed? To a person who is considering such a move. He is told: "Know that loneliness is a hard thing. Even those who are strong during the day, are weak at night, and the tears that they store up in their heart all day, sometimes as a game of strength, burst though their barriers at night. The stones of the walls of their home will be the only ones to hear, the only true witnesses to the depth of the tragedy. And that itself is terrible – for the stones of the Altar that are entrusted with bringing peace between man and his fellow, and between man and his G-d, feel that they have failed and have not fulfilled their mission, and they cry for all those whose weeping cannot even be heard.

I am sorry for writing so forthrightly that which is in my heart; but maybe somehow I'll be able to convince the two of you to reconsider.

I was happy to see that you felt good last night in HaMakom; not that you told me, but it's clearly visible when a person has attained a higher state. I hope that at least you will feel, during this difficult period you're undergoing, a sense of support or home in this place. I know that the motivation of the people of HaMakom is pure, without self-interest, and they truly want to do good for people and for the world.

With prayers for your success in all your struggles, and may G-d give you strength and good counsel and guidance,

–Meir

Nov. 12, 2009 14:22

Hi Meir,

Thanks for your email, and for praying for me too. It truly is nice to know that someone, somewhere, is thinking about you. It moved me. No matter what, we've had four nice years together, full of experiences.

Unfortunately, the matter with Atarah is final, at least for now. When we get a chance to talk I'll elaborate further. But it's something that cannot be bridged.

Incidentally, you spoke about the hardships that divorce will mean for the child. I just wanted to comment that until now, Yuval has been the uniting factor – but I always fear that when he grows up, we will find ourselves being bored together... which is an escape from ourselves. Just to keep on going for his sake does not suit us.

I understand you. Maybe in your circles it's not this way. The way I see it, even a good thing sometimes reaches a point where you feel that it has exhausted itself. If you see a great movie, would you want to see it every day? We're separating peaceably, without anger and without fighting.

You're right, I felt great yesterday. HaMakom is like a place of pleasant refuge for me, especially during this period of uncertainty.

Peace,

Shmulik

CHAPTER 13

HOW LONG DOES IT TAKE A MAN TO BE "RIPE" FOR MARRIAGE?

Nov. 9, 2011 14:26

Hi Meir, how are you?

Regarding what we were talking about, it's like this: We're both happy together, but once again, I just don't know if she's the one. The truth is, I'm already getting pretty tired of searching. There are some real differences between us, and my feelings towards her are also not consistent: Sometimes it's really great, and sometimes I feel indifferent, that there's just nothing there. A friend of mine once told me that when it's the real thing, you just know it. So I'm messed up. Maybe you can write me something clear about this, give me some type of general guidelines? I feel that I'll end up telling her too that it's not it. And my fear is that I might never find peace, and that my hope to build a family and home is just not realistic.

Last Friday, I was a guest at your friend's family; I don't know if he told you. When he sang *Eshet Chayil*[52] before Kiddush (he has an amazing voice, by the way), first he looked at his wife, then he closed his eyes and sang with such concentration

---
[52] "Woman of Valor," Proverbs 31

and connection, that I knew: this is what I want, a home like this. I couldn't control myself, and in the middle I actually started tearing up. Quite awkward. Maybe it's because of my fear that this is a dream that may never come true.

–Shlomi

Nov. 9, 2011 14:55

My very dear Shlomi,

Do you remember you once told me about your relationship with Yifat, "It's true that we feel good together, but how can I be sure she's the one? There are another thousand like her in Tel Aviv! Why should I rush?" How much closer you are now to your dream than you were then, right?

It's not so nice to say, but I'm finally hearing from you an inner distress regarding the search. That's great! My Rosh Yeshiva, Rav Hadari, once told me, "You want to know when you'll find? When you decide that the time has come to stop looking; when you love the taste of the find more than the taste of the search." Shlomi, somewhere, someplace, there's a woman waiting just for you; she's actually been waiting since the day she was born. I believe that, and your tears are the glue that you were missing up to now to complete the bonding with her. Let them flow – all the way to her.

Is there something spiritual that you and she could do together, such as learning together, or a project of some type? Maybe it could be something connected to the artistic interests that you share, in an atmosphere of spirituality? If I remember correctly, you first met at an exhibition of yours, right? It could be anything, as long as you feel that you're cooperating on a high level. I personally think that there should be something in one's spouse that awakens your most inner side, the highest and most vibrant aspects, something that pulls you upwards. It need not be something "exciting," but something that brings out the best in you. The two of you must feel that when you're together, you can make progress in building your mutual spiritual world, and that you have a common language regarding the loftier aspects of your personalities. More than that: sometimes neither side can understand the exact details of what the other is experiencing, but yet has what Hassidut calls an "encompassing" grasp on the "spirit" and "atmosphere" that the other is living through.

I'd like to send you a nice poem entitled "Woman." It was written by Hillel Zeitlin, *hy"d*, a very well-known journalist in Warsaw and a most mysterious spiritual character. He was murdered in the Holocaust. I'll look for it and send it. Meanwhile, I'm praying for your success, both individually and jointly, and may G-d shine His countenance upon the two of you.

–Meir

Meir, how're you doing?

Thank you so much for your help. Maybe I'll speak to you in HaMakom.

We also have lots of problems on the simple level of getting along... I'm starting to understand that I'm simply not ready yet, even though I very much want to be. I feel that this also affects the spiritual progress that I've made of late, with its ups and downs - mainly downs. Obviously I'll keep you posted on the developments. Thank you, thank you, and again thank you!

–Shlomi

Nov. 10, 2011

Dear Shlomi,

I hope I didn't mess up anything in our talk.

At what age is a person "ripe" for marriage? Do you want to wait until you're 40??

Personally, I've been saying for years that I'm still not sufficiently ready for my professional-arts field. That's why I keep on taking more classes and workshops and the like. Someone once told me, "Death always comes before perfection" – and this is a rule that has no exceptions.

I agree with you that you have some personal work to do and take care of, as we spoke about. But your tendency to take a break every time a problem comes up seems to me more like an "escape" than "work."

In any event, if you have reached such a strong level of clarification, it's all for the best; that's the best progress you can make. Marriage and life-partnership is not like food, which you cook and then eat; it's something that you keep working on and improving on as you go along, just like all of life. When I was a youth, I had some talks with Rabbi Mordechai Sternberg, a very great Torah scholar. He was teaching then in Yeshivat Merkaz HaRav, and today he's one of the Roshei Yeshiva of Yeshivat Har HaMor. I used to go to him for general advice about life and to show him some Torah thoughts I had written. He once told me, "On the face of it, it would have been better had man been given several years of preparation for life before embarking upon life itself. How can you use something before reading the instructions carefully? But G-d built the world totally differently, so I guess that theory is not correct. Apparently, there really is no proper order, and there is no set time that marks the end of preparation and the beginning of usage. And that's how it is in every area of life."

In general, to help you stabilize your progress in spirituality and worship of G-d, I think it would be a good idea to establish a framework, such as a synagogue or community to which you can be regularly connected. It would be good if, for instance, you could pray one prayer each day in the same place, a place where you feel good; the people there don't matter as much as the permanent "meeting" with G-d. And of course, it would be great to try to find a compatible study-partner on a regular basis. For you know that when you first started on the process of becoming a *baal teshuvah*, or however you would like to call it, you were all starry-eyed and full of enthusiasm. But now you have to face the day-to-day challenges, so just like in everything, a framework is a must.

Praying for your success,

–Meir

WOMAN

by Hillel Zeitlin
(a literal translation)

The Holy One, Blessed be He, said to the woman: "Be you to the man a shadow on his right hand, a symbol of soul, Divine Presence on earth /

And the man will see you as the most important thing: a crown of splendor, grace, pleasantness, softness, compassion, song, dream, his heart's yearning, and hope. /

And the man will see you and your image spread before him always, as a symbol of heavenly life on earth./

And the man will see you and you will be in his eyes a marker and sign of the supreme attribute of Splendor./

And the man will see you and you will be in his eyes the symbol of the mother of the world, giving life to all and spirit to her chosen sons. /

And the man will see you and you will be in his eyes the symbol of freedom, symbol of world aspirations, symbol of creativity and of striving that never ceases./

And the man will call in your name to wisdom, to music, to song, and to the daughters of the song./

And you will see the man steeped in catastrophes, troubles, day-to-day worries, and I will bestow upon you of My beauty and My mercies, and I will place your favor in his eyes, and he will forget his toil and his troubles./

And you will see the man steeped in sins, in failings, in the 49 gates of impurity, and I will bestow upon you from My glory, and you will raise up the man and extricate him from the gates of impurity to light, in the light of life."/

And the Holy One further said:

"If the man does not desire to see you, the beauty of your soul, but rather your body – you will become a curse for him./

He will then seek your closeness and will not find you, and he will consume his body and heart, and his spirit will be destroyed – and he will not find you./

And you will make yourself present for him for a moment, and he will never be satiated – as death is never satiated – and his days will be filled with the pangs of lust, jealousy, and hatred, war and competition./

And you will cause him to go astray, with your trickery, your light-headedness, your rashness, your narrowness of heart and smallness of soul, and you will ensnare him in your trap./

And he will be a slave to you forever, and he will go crazy from everything he sees and everything he hears, and he will constantly seek out new faces and new enjoyments, and will acquire new masters every day./

And I will place enmity between you and the man all the days of your life: He will lead you astray and you will lead him astray; he will kill your spirit, and you will poison every moment of his life... He will have many women and will not see *the* woman. /

And his heart and his flesh will pine always, and he will never know beauty. /

And he will acquire lust for women and the amusements of women, and will never know love..."

CHAPTER 14

FAITH IN THE FACE OF DEATH AND SUFFERING

Dear Meir, Post-Sabbath greetings!

First of all, I was sorry to miss the last meeting. Based on the title you gave it, I really missed something.

I would like to share with you something personal. Three years ago, I lost my mother, who died young of very torturous, cursed cancer. Her loss left a deep pit within me, for I was her only child living in Israel. My sister has lived abroad for many years and didn't really keep in touch with her. I became very attached to my mother, and tended her for four difficult years. While my friends spent their single years in fun trips abroad, having a good time, and worrying about nothing, I dealt with cardinal questions such as whether to remove a growth via an operation or with radiation, and the like. She underwent dozens of operations, treatments of different types, alternative therapies - and in the end, as I said, she died in sorrow.

When she became sick, I decided to make an unwritten deal with the Creator: I would observe Shabbat, and He would cure my mother. I was careful for almost a year to keep the Sabbath, I read Psalms, and I visited various Rabbis. I didn't succeed in my religious commitments, but I was left with a great craving for spiritual nourishment. I'm now trying to reach faith from a deeper source, but in the background I still "bear a grudge" that He did not relieve my mother of her tribulations. She was a good and upright woman, and she did not "deserve" it. I know that this is childish thinking, but I'm still a little girl in some ways... What do you think of all this in terms of religious faith?

I hope have not offended your religious sensibilities as a religious person.

Thanks in advance,

Ortal

Ortal, Shalom!

I read your letter and could barely believe it! Who can ever know what other people are going through!? You seem to be the happiest person around, full of strength and abilities – and now I don't know if it's despite what you went through, or because of it!

I certainly will not serve as G-d's defense counsel; He doesn't need me, nor anyone else, I imagine, for that. I don't have answers. But I would like to help you focus: What would you like to do with this now? What are your alternatives? "I am angry with You, and therefore– " what? You feel pain and loss and loneliness and longing and despair, and therefore you'll punish yourself with even more loneliness and detachment and anger? Living a life of anger and bitterness is not really an option, of course. Living like that leads nowhere other than to self-destruction. Obviously we would all like to understand more, and to know why things happen. It is clear that this lack of understanding makes it harder to live a life of faith. But, as King David writes in Psalms, *"Where shall I flee from Your presence? If I ascend to the heavens - You are there! And if I make my bed in the nethermost depths - behold, You are there!"* I have nowhere to run, no place is devoid of Your presence; this is the fact, whether I like it or not. Shall I live a spiritual, heavenly life without You? It doesn't work, it's lacking, and I'll end up anyway with You, the Source of Perfection. And if I simply surrender to deathly despair in This World – You are there as well; I'll meet up with You again with all the downtrodden and suffering, in the depths of man's suffering. I am weak, created, deficient, temporal, and I am in need of connection with eternity. I need close individual Divine providence, whether it be for good or for what appears bad to the mortal eye; I need to know that I am not just detached. I need to know that I didn't simply get on some train traveling from one unknown to another, and that at some point no one will just pluck me from my seat and throw me out to the four winds. It's impossible to live here in this world without faith in "goodness," without faith that there is reason and purpose to everything we are undergoing here.

From amidst your positive thinking, I can infer some good things about you. You have struggled with the real questions of life, whilst your friends escaped them, as you said. You were occupied with one of the most important *mitzvot* [Torah commandments]: Honor Thy Mother. Think about the illness as a given, and about your mother being sick without your support, Heaven forbid. Aren't such thoughts so much more dreadful? I'll tell you something personal of my own. My late mother also passed away from that same disease. My brother tended her when she was sick with tremendous dedication. He refused to have a helper come in to take care of her, because even though it was so terribly difficult for him to see his beloved mother deteriorating before his eyes, he felt that this was the final and major kindness that he could do for her, and that this was the best thing for her. What greater goodness can a person do here in this world? I am convinced that the struggles you dealt with helped deepen your thoughts and emotions, and made you into a more understanding woman, a more attentive and sensitive wife, and with G-d's help, a better mother for your children.

When the Creator chose to create us as people with different emotions, He also implanted within us a finely-developed sense of justice, by which we rise up against what appears to us as injustice, and become angered and saddened by it. G-d even commanded us to cry over and eulogize the deceased. This means that we emphasize his or her good qualities, and thus imply that the world is now lacking because of this loss – yet in no way does this mean that we complain or rail against G-d. We do not presume to understand everything, for if we did, we would have no need for Him; we ourselves would be G-d. We have no need to suppress or conceal these feelings and questions, but rather just to live with them with humility.

I hope that with this lack of answer, I have answered something...

–Meir

To Meir, a precious man: Shalom and blessing.

You certainly answered. But I still do not fully understand you. I mean, I sense terrible injustice, and you believe that our feelings are true and correct. You don't say that we are forbidden to ask such questions, because they stem from the sense of justice that the Creator implanted within us. And you write that there is nowhere to escape. But what support can I find in a model of justice that I cannot accept? What support can I find in One Who does everything, including making my mother sick and having her die with suffering?

Again, I apologize for the sharp language.

–Ortal

Dear Ortal,

No need to apologize; I prefer straight and clear language.

So then, on whom *can* you rely? Is there anyone else who provides a better example of justice? And to remain without any support is impossible. You can choose to be furious over the suffering she endured, or you can choose to smile at the small favor He did by giving her you during those difficult hours. When we say "G-d," or call Him by any other name, we are essentially saying, "Perfection: the Perfection of beauty, of eternity, of love, of might, of kindness, and more - including also justice." If the justice you perceive is not sufficient, it means that you essentially believe in something even higher: the most absolute and perfect level of justice – what we call "G-d." Belief in such justice is imbued in us. After all, we are angered by injustice – proving that we believe in justice, for why else should we expect life to be just?

And so, the only thing that remains for us to do in the face of this "injustice" is to refine and uplift our imagination to a higher and more perfect place, to a place of absolute justice, even if it is inconceivable to us and higher than anything we could possibly imagine. This means, paradoxically, that the less a person understands, the more he believes; this is his innate need. We are permitted to say that we have no conception of the essence of eternity of the soul, and that we cannot begin to know the sublime value of suffering – though no one would ever choose it – in terms of its purification of our soul.

May it be His will that we not be tested with this type of test, and that we merit to see good in its most obvious form.

Good luck on your final exam, and please send warm regards to Yaniv.

-Meir

CHAPTER 15

WHY DO I ALWAYS GET THE YOM KIPPUR "I'VE SINNED, FORGIVE ME" BLUES?

Aug. 24, 2010 21:00

Dear Meir, Shalom!

There's a small synagogue near my house, and over the last few nights, I've noticed people coming really late, even at 1 AM, to pray. I asked someone what prayer this is, and he said it's *slichot*[53] recited before the Day of Atonement (Yom Kippur). So I wanted to ask you about these *slichot*, and about this "I sinned" that we keep on repeating on Yom Kippur. I get an uncomfortable feeling with the word "forgive" that is so much a part of those long Yom Kippur prayers, and with the guilt feelings that it brings on. What is this forgiveness? From whom are we asking for forgiveness, and for what? It's true that I'm secular - but I believe in G-d, I try not to hurt anyone, I try to honor my parents as much as I can, and I behave honestly and fairly (sometimes too much). Why do I need to walk around with these guilt feelings, with low self-esteem and self-confidence? I don't like the depressive

---

[53] in which we ask for *slichah*, forgiveness

atmosphere of this day, and of the days before it. On a different topic, my friend teaches 11th grade in a kibbutz high school, a regional school for all the kibbutzim of the area. She wants to give a class on *slichot*, with nice and interesting *midrashim* (homiletical texts), and connect them all to modern life. Given your familiarity with this field, I'm sure you could help and direct me to the right sources, whether sacred or secular texts. I'm sure she'll then be able to put together a lesson that will give a spiritual charge to secular students. So you see, I'm not as secular as you probably think...

–Ruth

Aug. 31, 2000

Dear Ruth,

The first *slichah* [singular of *slichot*] is that I'm sorry for responding so late...

I'll first answer your questions about the slichot, the guilt feelings and Yom Kippur. Relatively recent Jewish sources include different approaches regarding self-assessment. For instance:

1. The Mussar movement was started about 150 years ago with the purpose of improving man's ethical character. One of the sub-movements within the Mussar approach was known as Novardok; it was

practically wiped out during the Holocaust, and was not renewed. Novardok demanded of its adherents very critical self-inspection, and insisted that a person should not grant himself much credit. One who does not work hard to rectify his character traits, according to Novardok, is by definition not a "high quality" person. The verse that states "man's inclination of heart is bad from the days of his youth" means that one's natural inclination is towards the bad, and that he can reverse this only if he works hard on himself to moderate and refine his character. A person who does not "process" himself in this manner is more like an animal: egotistical, desirous of control, conquest, and self-indulgence, and with no ethical framework. Novardok holds that one must spend his life as if he is in constant debt, searching for what he has not yet rectified, without patting himself on the back for those aspects of his personality that he has fixed.

2. At the opposite extreme is the approach of Rav Kook, which has become quite accepted in modern times. It is that man is good, and that his task in the world is to uncover the goodness within him. As the Torah states, *"G-d made man straight."* The bad within him is not his real essence, but rather attests to a blockage in the way he actualizes his strengths and abilities. The way to character refinement, accordingly, is based on this view of our goodness.

3. In between these is the "middle" approach, found for instance in the Sefer HaTanya of Chabad, and

possibly in most of the Hassidic movement. It is also, in certain ways, the approach of the Slobodka school of the Mussar movement. Its source is in an interpretation of the Gemara and Maimonides, according to which one should generally view oneself as neither evil nor righteous, but rather as "medium" - in a perpetual struggle between his inclination to act ethically and his opposing tendency to the other direction.

Really the difference between these approaches is more one of tactics than of values and essence. That is, there is no dispute about the truth of the matter, but only about awareness. Each of the approaches is appropriate for one period or another. But even according to the "I'm OK" school, we must not allow our positive thinking to lead us to a state of irresponsibility, apathy and failure to work. A person must learn to recognize and ask forgiveness for what he did wrong, and to humble himself when necessary.

Once a year, around the days of Rosh HaShanah and Yom Kippur, we allow ourselves to feel our "spiritual orphanhood," as stated in this verse that we recite during the month of Elul before Rosh HaShanah: *"Though my father and mother have left me, G-d will gather me in."* These are days of appeasement and reconciliation, in which we focus on the empty half of the glass, on that which we have to yet work and improve. This process itself has beauty and softness – vis-à-vis both man and G-d; everything is softer. This period is not meant to depress us. On the contrary, we are given the opportunity to taste the sweet flavor of the fruit of inner cleanliness, to inhale the odor of purity. Just like the spring cleaning that people like to do before Passover, so that everything will be sparkling and new, so too with the spiritual cleanliness in the days of Elul and the Ten Days of Repentance. The work is occasionally a bit uncomfortable, but the resulting sensation is wonderful and unequalled.

The Yom Kippur prayers open with the *Shehecheyanu* blessing to Him Who has "given us life and subsistence, and has brought us to this time," and it is said with immense joy. Why? Because this is a day of happiness, of forgiveness and purity, of parting from all the vows and prohibitions and ropes with which we have bound ourselves all year – like the million thin threads that bound the giant Gulliver in the land of the dwarves. This is a day when we regret our mistakes and missed opportunities, when we take responsibility for not letting ourselves be who and what we really are. This is a day of separation from the routines that strangle our creativity, from our subjugation to social restraints that steal our lives from us. This is a day on which we remove all our pretenses, let go of the social image we have been projecting – an image to which we feel obligated. Sometimes we can even free ourselves of our own self-image. These are images with which we may have been stuck for years, preventing us from bursting forth towards realizing our own potential, to what we really have to do, to what is right for our soul. This is why, as an introduction to this blessing, we say, with great emotion, the *Kol Nidrei* prayer: "All our vows, and all that binds us, should be null and void." Only after we have freed ourselves from all the bonds and bans that we have created for ourselves, will we be free to live our lives without sin and without missing[54] our destiny.

I hope this somewhat eases your difficulties regarding Yom Kippur.

Regarding your friend and her teaching plans, I like the book "On Repentance" by Rabbi Dr. Yosef Soloveitchik. There is a very nice and relevant passage there[55] on King David's wife Avigayil's call to rouse ourselves from our daily routine, with the author's homiletic commentary.

She can read Chapter 8 of "The Little Prince," in which he confesses his sin in not understanding the rose. The reference is to the misunderstandings between man and woman, but also between ourselves and others in general, others who have a language and modes of behavior different from our own. And speaking of roses, there is a beautiful *piyut* (liturgical poem) in the *slichot* of Yom Kippur night that mentions a rose; the source of this imagery is Shir HaShirim, Song of Songs. Every line in this *piyut* ends with the sweet word, "I have forgiven."

---

[54] The Hebrew for "sin" and "missing" in this case come from the same root chet-tet-aleph.

[55] p. 218 in the Hebrew edition

And of course, the poem "Slichot" by Leah Goldberg can be taken in different directions. I feel in it something very primeval, something of childhood sensations. Here's an interesting exercise: What would happen if we think of the subject of this poem as a dialogue and a link with G-d, as a prayer? Something to think about...

There is a nice story by I. L. Peretz[56] about a *slichot* session with the Rebbe of Riminov, with some indirect commentary on the innovations of Hassidut. It has beauty to it, and a positive outlook on people, noting that one can never know from the outside what the other is really about. The story is titled, "If Not Higher."

Regarding the structure of the *slichot*: They center around the Thirteen Divine Attributes of Mercy (Exodus 34), which are among the secrets G-d revealed to Moses regarding how He guides and leads the world. There are countless commentaries and Midrashim on these attributes. The passage is recited repeatedly like a refrain, in all Jewish congregations the world over. The *piyutim* were composed over the course of many years, 1,000 years ago or so, and are not necessarily the same in all communities.

Ideas for class exercises:

1. Dealing with forgiveness: asking a friend for forgiveness, the difficulty involved, overcoming it,

---

[56] Yiddish- and Hebrew-language author and playwright, considered among the greatest classical Yiddish writers and one who helped revolutionize modern Hebrew literature

and the joy of "liberation" after it happens. (There are three steps, as the Baal Shem Tov explains: submission; differentiation [between bad and good]; and sweetening [the difficulty]).

2. Dealing with forgiving someone else. Have you ever found yourself in this situation? Were you able to truly forgive? How did you do it?

3. Dealing with the *slichot* on the religious/ethical/ conscience levels, with feelings of guilt, and the process of understanding that is necessary for erasing/ atonement/release, for self-forgiveness. How can we "inscribe ourselves" in the Divine Ledger – as mentioned in *Un'taneh Tokef*, one of the most profound passages in the High Holiday prayers – without faking it or lying to ourselves? This is where we simply stand and face the great truth.

I wish you great success in this challenge, and to all of us - a good High Holiday inscription for life and goodness!

–Meir

CHAPTER 16

HOPES AND MIRACLES FOR ONE WHO IS CRITICALLY ILL

Oct. 13, 2009 15:27

Hi Meir,

How are you? I enjoy the titles you give to your weekly classes, even though I don't actually manage to get there to take part...

I have a very big personal favor to ask of you. My cousin was injured in a car accident, and I ask with all my heart that you pray for him. He is in very bad shape and we really need prayers, blessings, and good thoughts around him and for him. His name is --.

And on this topic I wanted to ask you: I heard that there's something called "name-changing" for one who is very sick. Is this the right thing to do? And if so, how do we go about it?

Thanks very much in advance, from me and our family, and I hope that we will soon return to our routine.

Thank you,

Keren

Oct. 13, 2009 18:08

Dear Keren,

...May he have a speedy and complete recovery. The best prayer is that of relatives and friends, because it stems from their deepest desires. Of course, all other prayers also help.

At times, according to the Kabbalists, the name of one who is sick is changed. This is based on our knowledge that one's name is also one's essence, and therefore if his name is changed, he is no longer the same person upon whom the suffering was decreed. It might also symbolize a deep change in his life altogether after he recovers, with G-d's help, when he will be as if born anew. But of course this must be kept in proportion: It is not a fundamental principle of Judaism, and in fact it's much more important to make sure that he receives the best medical care possible. His parents are certainly busy with that, and it wouldn't be right to "bother" them at this time with this spiritual matter.

I hope that aside from this, you [plural] are doing well, and are making progress in what is important to you. Regards to Avi!

–Meir

P.S. I remembered now that today is the 200th anniversary of the death of Rabbi Levi Yitzchak of

Berditchev, who was known as the "public defender of Israel." We once talked about him, if you remember. He was a person whose abundant optimism could cure the sick and turn difficult situations totally around. He had what we now call "boundless positive energies."

Oct. 14, 2009

Hi Meir,

Thanks very much for your good intentions. We're hoping and praying that he will wake up from his coma.

Regarding the name: Yes, it's a bit sensitive right now, but it will certainly come up in the future. I wrote you about it because a friend of mine at work keeps telling me that it's urgent for us to change the name, and go to the grave of a certain righteous man who is buried near the Knesset, and that I should not let up on his parents on this matter – so you helped me calm down.

Thanks for everything, from all my heart, and I hope to update you with happy developments.

–Keren

March 8, 2010 23:46

Dear Keren,

... I hope you had a joyous Purim. I myself was fairly inebriated[57], very happy and free, but I can remember every detail. As opposed to Yom Kippur, when I am a cantor and have a responsibility towards the gabbai (sexton) and all the worshipers – on Purim, there's hardly any of that "formality." I had a good prayer, a direct prayer. And then I remembered your cousin and his condition, and that he apparently still needs many prayers, because otherwise you would have told me.

This morning, I ran to catch a bus, but missed it – and someone from the neighborhood saw me and stopped to give me a ride. I asked him how he was doing, and he smiled and said, "Every day that I'm in this world, it's a miracle." He explained that some weeks ago he underwent open heart surgery, and then two days later suffered a severe stroke, leaving him unconscious and paralyzed on his entire left side. He was in the Shaarei Tzedek hospital, there was no improvement, and so they decided to transfer him to Hadassah Ein Karem for brain surgery. His room was adjacent to that of Rabbi Mordechai Eliyahu[58], may he be well. His family members approached Rav

---

[57] in keeping with the Purim practice of rejoicing and drinking at least more than one is accustomed to...

[58] former Chief Sephardic Rabbi of Israel and a great Kabbalist; he died in 2010 after a long illness

Eliyahu and asked him to pray for him. The Rav blessed him and murmured some prayers for about three
minutes; they couldn't hear what he was saying. The
Rabbi then asked his students who were there to sing
"Bar Yochai." The hospital staff meanwhile arrived to
get him [my benefactor driver] ready for his operation. Rav Eliyahu's guys are singing, it's only 15 minutes until the operation, and the man's wife sees her
husband mumbling the words of the refrain of "Bar
Yochai" along with them. She runs to Rav Eliyahu's
wife to tell her, the doctors come to check, and the
man in fact wakes up. The boys then hesitate in their
singing, afraid to disturb the patient, but the Rav says
no, they should keep on singing more. It very soon
became clear that the man was no longer paralyzed,
and the operation was called off. This is the story told
me by the man driving me, the very man to whom it
happened.

What does it mean? I don't know. I thought about
Rav Eliyahu, who has been ill for a couple of years,
and who keeps going back and forth from this world
to the next, there and back again, almost every few
days. (I heard from a professor on the medical staff
treating him that he wanted to write a medical article
about this so-rare phenomenon that Rabbi Eliyahu is
undergoing, but he decided against it for fear that no
one would believe him and he would become a laugh-
ingstock. He said there are apparently people whose
bodies, and not only their souls, function differently

than what scientific research dictates. I know the man well, he is widely admired and a rationalist.

Why am I telling you all this? I have no understanding regarding miracles; you can never know the absolute truth regarding these stories, and it's likely that there are exaggerations. But on the other hand, "there's no smoke without fire..." I thought it might do you and your family good to know that strange things do happen in this world, including miracles. There's still hope!

Be blessed,
Meir

Hi Meir,

Thank you for sharing that story with me about the rabbi, it really does gladden the heart and offer hope. The story is very interesting. Is there a way I can reach that rabbi? Maybe with his help, my cousin, too, can be saved...

Good night,
Keren

June 8, 2010 16:48

Dear Keren,
I hope all is well and streaming in constructive directions.

Regarding Rav Eliyahu and the phone number of his relative that I sent you at the time, as you asked – I don't know if you were able to do something with it or not. In general, I don't think that salvation comes via one specific person. We all have the privilege of being able to turn to G-d directly. But it is clear that there are people who have special prayer strengths. I myself don't understand a thing in these matters. Not long ago I had to accompany someone to an operation in Shaarei Tzedek, where Rav Eliyahu was hospitalized. I thought I could get over to him and give him a note with your cousin's name and a request for prayer. But in the end, I was so involved with my friend's operation that I couldn't leave even for a moment, and the opportunity to approach Rav Eliyahu, or his family members, was lost.

As you have surely heard, Rav Eliyahu passed away yesterday. I had not seen such a large funeral for many years – more than 100,000 people, of all types and striped, gathered together within a matter of hours. People were talking, and everyone had a personal story to tell. It is fascinating that when I talked with people about him during his long period of illness, and also at the funeral, almost everyone said that the Rav had a special place in his heart for him or her. Everyone seemed to feel that he, more than anyone else, had a uniquely close relationship with him. I think I heard that hundreds of times. Pretty nice, no? Tomorrow I would like to dedicate part of the class to

a talk about the man and what he accomplished.
All the blessings,
Meir

Sep. 6, 2010

Hi,

No, I don't remember how, but somehow it was pushed off and we never got in touch with him... I am sad to hear that we missed our last chance to have him possibly help us. The strangest thing is that I don't remember ever having heard his name in the past. You were the first to tell me about him. Why is this? Are we, the seculars, really such ignoramuses about what's going on in the religious world? There is a religious man in my workplace, and I asked him if he ever heard of Rav Eliyahu. He said, "Of course! I used to consult with him on everything, he was like my father." Sometimes I think that we're living in two different, far-away countries, even when we're in the same little land, and maybe even in the same office. It makes me curious to want to learn much more, to get to know. I have this suspicion that someone in the educational system purposely made sure to prevent us from knowing all these things, to hide all this information about Judaism, for some unknown reason, and the same thing happens in the media. The religious people that

I meet in real life are very different than those on
TV. How do you explain this?
    –Keren

CHAPTER 17

CAN A WOMAN WEAR TEFILLIN?

Aug. 9, 2012

Hi Meir, how are you? I greatly enjoyed your class yesterday on subconscious imagery in our dreams. I walked home along the beach so I could have more time to think about it and digest it.

I was reading this morning in Deuteronomy, in the portion of Ekev, if I'm not mistaken, or maybe Vaetchanan – and I read about mezuzah and tefillin. I started wondering: Are women also permitted to put on tefillin? I ran some searches in Google, and I didn't find any blanket prohibition or any specific law that says it's forbidden.

What I did find is that the Shulchan Arukh has reservations about it, but I can't seem to understand if that means it's clearly forbidden. I would assume that during menstruation, it is not allowed. But I would like to know if the rest of the time it is forbidden by Halakhic ruling from the Torah or the Gemara, or if it's just a custom that has taken root.

Thanks very much,

Drorit

Aug. 9, 2012 16:15

Drorit, Shalom!

Regarding the tefillin, first of all, it brings me joy to see your enthusiasm in seeking out closeness to G-d. Sometimes, people who grew up with a religious education become a bit jaded, whereas your excitement is fresh and dynamic!

Secondly, I would be very interested in pinpointing your motivation to wear tefillin. That is, it's clear that a woman is not obligated to put on tefillin, and the question is only whether she may do so voluntarily. The question that this raises is: What arouses a person to seek to fulfill a mitzvah that he is not required to do? Is it a matter of a "feeling"? Perhaps it's a social statement? I read many years ago a work of Halakhic responsa in which a woman had asked about tzitzit and tefillin, and the answer was that she could wear tzitzit under her clothing without it showing at all, if it's very important to her, but that she should not wear tefillin even in private. Another rabbi ruled that women may don tefillin only privately. Why is this? Because these questions often stem from elements who are trying to destabilize or mock the Halakhic system, and not from pure Halakhic motivations. Sometimes they seek to make a defiant political statement, and that's why even the more lenient decisor qualified his ruling by requiring that it not be used to advance political interests.

This is clearly not the case here; yours is just a private matter and not a social one. What remains, then, is just to understand this point: What is your personal motivation? What does it involve, what can be gained from it, and what does it lead to? Clarifying these points will enable me to better relate to your question.

In general, one is permitted to "volunteer" to perform a mitzvah in which he or she is not obligated. For instance, a woman can fulfill the mitzvah of the Four Species (lulav, etc.) on Sukkot. But when it comes to clothing and the like, we meet up with the Torah prohibition of men wearing women's garments and vice-versa. Each gender must not seek to be like the other. A person should be at peace with his or her self-identity in every sense, and should not imitate another person, group, or phenomenon. Therefore the question here - which I don't presume to answer - is whether a woman wearing tefillin, even in private, presents an issue of her dressing like a man.

But there is another point to be raised here: When a person wants to achieve closeness to G-d and higher levels of sanctity, we may ask whether he is already fulfilling all that he is commanded to do! Before he runs to volunteer for extra service, has he completed his basic requirements? Consider, for instance, a father who performs kindnesses and helps everyone, and then has no time for his children – is that logical and right?

Incidentally, the author of the work Arukh HaShulchan (not to be confused with the Shulchan Arukh) notes that even men today do not wear tefillin all day, as was originally the practice, but only for the minimum required time – and so therefore one who is not obligated at all should certainly not be stringent and wear them! But I don't think we have to go into this interesting point at this time.

Again, I'm only trying to understand, and am writing simply to ask.

–Meir

Aug. 9, 2012 22:24

Hi Meir.

The reason I asked about women wearing tefillin is that it interests me on a personal level; I would like to wear tefillin alone in my own apartment (not every day, but maybe occasionally), out of a sense that this will bring me spiritually closer to G-d. I have heard that it is a unique experience, and I would like to try it. I once read an article about halo-colors that envelop different people, and it claims (with photographic proof) that the halo around someone wearing tefillin looks purple – which is the highest and most spiritual halo. So this means that wearing tefillin is an experience of holiness or something like it. It certainly has nothing to do with social statements by Reform Jews or the like.

If there is no specific prohibition, then I can't see why I shouldn't do it. But if it's because of specific laws that must be studied, I would be happy to know what they are.

Thank you,

Drorit

Aug. 9, 2012 22:51

Drorit, Shalom.

The commandments in Judaism are not for the purpose of granting experiences, whether they be spiritual, emotional, or intellectual. It's not that the mitzvot lack positive experiences of this type –but this is not their purpose. Mitzvot must be fulfilled for their own sake, simply because they were commanded. Doing them for this purpose is what forms our connection with G-d and bring us closer to Him.

Let's say a man wants to buy his wife a birthday gift, to express his love and appreciation for her. She loves books, and could easily gladden her with a nice new book. But it would be more "fun" for him to buy her a CD of music that he himself likes. "After all," he thinks as he tries to convince himself, "she also likes music to a certain extent. And what's wrong with me also enjoying her gift? Don't I deserve a little something too? It's not like she did more than me in order to be born; 'just because another year has passed, for that she deserves a gift[59]?'... And she certainly won't suffer from hearing this music, she actually likes it, sometimes, even though she might like other types of music even more..."

Sometimes this is what the fulfillment of mitzvot in our generation looks like. At times we choose our priorities in Halakhah based on what we would like to "experience." We should not confuse between the mitzvah itself and what it "feels" like.

Yes, there is definitely an "experiential" aspect of fulfilling mitzvot. But the most fundamental aspect thereof is "doing what G-d wants, the way He wants," as He expressed it in the Torah. It of course doesn't matter whether what He wants appears to us to be reasonable or not. If He wants us not to mix meat and milk, or to blow the shofar, then that is our commandment. For the husband mentioned above, he would achieve a beautiful experience of closeness and friendship with his wife if he were to succeed in making her truly happy on her birthday according to her own desires, no matter how "strange" they may seem to him.

If, after and despite everything I have written, you still feel a burning desire to wear tefillin, let's talk and try to clarify the matter.

–Meir

---

[59] Based on the song "Birthday prayer", by Tirtza Atar.

CHAPTER 18

IS THE TORAH'S APPROACH TO HOMOSEXUALITY PRIMITIVE?
AND, CAPITAL PUNISHMENT IN THE TORAH

Aug. 2, 2015 19:19

Hi Meir,

I've been in shock the past few days at what happened at the Gay Pride march in Jerusalem[60]. The religious people will once again say that the killer is just a crazy extremist on the fringe of religious society, and that there shouldn't be such a march in Jerusalem, and the like. I grew up in a religious home, arguably even hareidi; I learned in a Yeshiva a bit, and I'm familiar with everything. I've heard from you in HaMakom a different tune, so maybe I'll hear something new from you on this topic too. I never spoke to a rabbi about this, it would be awkward, but I'm not embarrassed to ask you.

The truth is that my older sister's son was there at the parade, he himself is gay, and now I find myself being attacked by him because I was once religious! Absurd, no? He has strong questions,

---

[60] On July 30, 2015, a 40-year-old man stabbed seven people at the Jerusalem gay pride march, including a 16-year-old girl whose wounds were fatal. The murderer was ultimately sentenced to life plus 31 years in prison, as well as a fine of approximately $650,000 in damages.

and I've become your defender! So let me ask simply and clearly:

1. Why should someone be faulted for being born with a different sexual inclination? Does Judaism say that he must suffer all his life because of the inclination with which he was born?

2. Why did the Creator, Who according to Judaism is compassionate and merciful, issue in the Torah the death penalty for someone who sinned in this, even assuming it's a sin?

Thanks,

Yaron

Dear Yaron, Shalom!

The questions you raise have nothing at all to do with the murder, which is covered in the Ten Commandments by two simple words: Lo tirtzach, "Do not murder!" Totally straightforward, there's nothing to add, and it has nothing to do with fringe elements or anything else: There is no connection at all between murder and Judaism. It's quite unanimous, all agree that murder is forbidden. There is only one Jewish Law, one Rambam, one Shulchan Arukh.

Having emphasized that point, I would like to relate to the topic of the Torah's approach to homosexuality, as I understand it, step by step.

"Therefore shall a man leave his father and mother and unite with his wife and become one flesh"

(Genesis 2:24). Thus begins the story of man-and-wife relations in the world, according to the Torah. Rashi explains: "What makes them become one flesh? How can two people become one? – Via their common offspring." Though it's not popular to say so in some modern circles, a child marks the completion of the relationship. The offspring is not separate from the parents' relationship, and certainly does not mar it. This is the Jewish outlook on the wholeness of marriage: without a child, it is not complete.

The concept of our obligation to the environment and the continued existence of the world is not a modern invention. It rather appears in the second chapter of the Bible: "… to work it and preserve it" (2:15). We have a moral obligation vis-à-vis the world, and cannot simply use-and-dispose of it. It is our responsibility to sustain the world. A relationship without children does not build or sustain the world, but is rather an inward focus on one's own personal needs. Prospective spouses may take time to build and deepen their relationship, but in general, the direction must be towards having children.

The Torah anchors this view in its commandments, of which one is to marry and have children. One who is unable to fulfill this commandment is exempt, for he has no choice in the matter. But there is also another Torah injunction: "Do not lie with a man as one would with a woman; this is an abomination" (Lev. 18:22). That is, if someone wants to do this or is drawn to it – the Torah forbids it. No one wants to do this if he is not drawn to it, and therefore the Torah is speaking specifically to him. This tells us that the Torah acknowledges that there are those who are drawn to it – and it forbids them from acting on it. The prohibition is not on having this attraction – no one is blamed for that – but rather on the action, which the Torah says is very bad.

Incidentally, the Torah also relates very critically to physical male-female relations that are not directed towards building a relationship. All relations involving sexual exploitation, objectification, or a marring of the sanctity of the act of intercourse – "wasteful expulsion of semen," such as Er and Onan did (Genesis 38:7-9) – is bad in G-d's eyes.

It is true that this presents an extra-difficult test for one who has this tendency. But it is precisely this idea that "one must try out everything he is attracted to" that has brought our modern world to such a low ethical level.

One may try to philosophize as to why the Torah forbade this act, and why it terms it a to'evah, an abomination ["disgusting" or "perverse," according to other translations], and how the Sages explained it. Many of the sources tell us that sexual relations should express encouragement, closeness and love. However, in our generation love and desire have been separated, and thus love has been lost.

Jewish Law suffices with simply "forbidding"

lesbianism, but male homosexuality is actually called a to'evah. There are sources in the Midrash, Kabbala and Talmud to the effect that a soul connection is strengthened by sexual relations that express closeness and love, where each partner gives pleasure to the other in an act of mutual and simultaneous pleasure. This is a very high level of connection.

But all this is just a possible approach by which to understand the depth of the matter. As a general rule, the very attempt to empower a relationship that does not truly connect the two partners, that does not strive for the highest form of connection, is a desecration of holiness. The sanctity of the covenant of marriage - the pre-eminence of the love act - is desecrated when it is brought down to a low level. But regarding the love between a man and wife on a high level, R. Akiva said: "All the songs are holy, but the Song of Songs is the Holy of Holies[61]."

In order to distance us from anything close to this type of desecration, the Torah was very strict in this area, and not only regarding homosexuality. The latter is just an example, but any other act that does not strengthen the spiritual connection is regarded just as severely.

Of course, the Torah does not relate negatively to those who have this attraction, and we are bidden

---

[61] Song of Songs, one of the 24 books of the Bible, deals with spouses' deep search for each other, with the extreme expressions of love, and with the most intimate relationship between man and woman. This Song also serves as a parable for the secret of love between G-d and the Congregation of Israel.

"not to judge your fellow until you have been in his place." The problem is that a society that regards having children as just another hobby, like tennis or stamp-collecting, is that which idealizes homosexual bonds. A society that has come to spurn the value of family – a sacred, meaningful, existential value – and whose members would not even be alive had their parents not believed in the concept of family, thus paves the way towards the replacement of the traditional family with this new, sterile structure.

One of the issues in dispute today is whether same-sex couples have the right to public funding to enable them to raise children. Many ethical questions come into play here. How do we define whose child is whose? That is, if the sperm is not his, and the egg - and possibly even the womb - is not hers, in what way are they considered parents? Are we going to start merchandising children? Today the biological father is in a relationship with one man, and established a "family" – but if tomorrow they break up, what connection will remain between the child and the man he grew up thinking was his (non-biological) "parent"? And even if we acknowledge that some of these issues are also present in adoption or second marriages, when the pregnancy does not happen in the normal way, is this not a significant factor in parentage? And does not every child to be raised by one intimate mother, as well as one father? Do we deem nature to be so gravely mistaken? Can a man be

Divine and engineer the entire world according to his will? Is this not a symptom of egotistical hedonism, harm to a child simply so that a person can enjoy the experience of parenthood? Is life nothing more than just a collection of personal experiences, with no obligation to anyone else? This is not Judaism. The main principle of Judaism is rather to think about and consider the other's needs: "Love your neighbor like yourself."

You ask, "Why should someone be faulted for being born with a different sexual inclination?" You're right; he's not at fault. Judaism is all compassion and love, and does not seek to place blame. Precisely for this reason, should we allow him, just because he is suffering, to cause suffering to others? Because he is suffering, should he be permitted to do something unethical?

We have a principle: "G-d does not try a person with a test that he cannot withstand." He gives very difficult tests – and for some people, perhaps the stronger ones, the tests are even harder. These people must therefore look for ways to overcome them. What should one do who never married because he couldn't find a wife and who lives his entire life alone? Does the Torah permit him that which is forbidden to everyone else?

Of course, all these explanations cannot mollify one who is suffering. Even the Talmudic Sages rejected suffering and tribulations that might merit them some extra reward: "No thanks, we want neither the suffering nor its reward," they said. The only thing we can do, sometimes, is simply to lament together with him...

One thing that is clear is that the public discourse is actually able to create a given reality, and not just relate to it from the side. Today's extremist discourse has already impaired the free choice of many who find themselves torn regarding their attractions. There are those who have a "partial" attraction to members of their own gender, and would definitely be able to form a normal relationship and have children – if it weren't for modern society's stubborn demand to put clear and distinct labels on everyone. Forcing them to categorize themselves on one side or the other is very difficult for them. If, for instance, they would want to try therapy that they believe could possibly help them, wouldn't the very discussion of such definitions spoil any effort to this end? Don't we have sufficient compassion towards people who suffer to let them alone to deal with their struggle in a straightforward manner? Why must young teenagers be subjected to the complexities of "defining their sexual identity"?

I feel that this is a problem in many areas of life. I know a girl with great musical talent whose music teacher "put her in a box" by saying, "You just don't have what it takes to be a musician" – and the girl thereupon abruptly stopped her musical studies.

Though the preoccupation with definitions is

harmful, it is reasonable to assume that one's commitment to Jewish Law minimizes this phenomenon, as it does not relate to homosexuality as a practical option.

Regarding your questions about capital punishment in the Torah:

Already two millennia ago, when the Sanhedrin was the top court in ancient Israel, it was considered a "killer" court if it executed even one person in 70 years. Other Sages said that had they sat on the Sanhedrin, capital punishment would never have been carried out. We all know that in other countries, including some exemplary democracies, the execution rate is many times higher than once in 70 years. Even in Israel, in its some 70 years of existence, more people have been killed…

Why is this? For a death sentence to be carried out, the guilty party must, apparently, want very much to die: Two valid witnesses must see a very specific act, they must warn him precisely that if he commits the crime he will be punished by death, and he must be entirely aware and even acknowledge that he knows he is liable for death and is doing it anyway. And even then the court will always seek out points in his favor. In addition, some opinions hold that no evidence can always be 100%, since no one can see an entire act, etc. In short, the whole concept of a death sentence in Judaism is essentially theoretical.

202 • Twice In Love - Meir Dorfman

In the waning days of the Sanhedrin, it abolished the death penalty altogether, and today, when there is no Sanhedrin, there certainly can be no death sentences.

Why then does the Torah say about certain crimes that the perpetrator must *"certainly be put to death?"* The Torah wishes to express its essential position on the severe ethical gravity of these sins.

The sanctity of life is one of the most sublime values in the entire Torah. We can only wish and hope that Western society would adopt even a small fraction of the sacred view of life that exists in Judaism.

As a rule, Judaism does not emphasize punishment. It believes not in sinking into the mire of evil, but rather demands immediate rectification. If one must be distanced from society, he is sent not to jail, but to a "city of refuge," where many Levite and Torah scholars reside and where he can learn from them and improve his ways. In prison, on the other hand, people generally become close to and are influenced by other criminals. Even monetary fines are few in number, teaching us that one must relate to his fellow's money most carefully, and be totally cautious not to take what is not his or to cause damage – for not every damage can be repaired.

Incidentally, how sad it is that people think that Judaism is exactly the opposite of what it actually is. Why should anyone even suspect that murdering a girl at a gay pride march is mandated by the Torah?

Is it just because the murderer has a beard and yarmulke? It is simply ignorance of what Judaism is all about. Handing down the laws and values of Torah from generation to generation via those who study it is the very essence of Judaism; has anyone ever heard a learned Torah scholar speak in violent terms? Does a G-d-fearing Jew ever do anything without asking what Jewish Law says about it? And certainly not in matters of life and death! To think otherwise is simply ignorance.

Yaron, I have tried to review the topic from many angles. Of course, if I were to speak with your nephew, I would relate to him more personally.

See you,

Meir

CHAPTER 19

"AND G-D WAS ANGERED" – WHAT, IS HE A MORTAL??

Oct. 21, 2012 19:24

Dear Alon,

You asked me something during class and I couldn't answer, because in truth, such questions require almost an entire lesson on their own.

A. You are puzzled by the descriptions of G-d in the Torah, as if He has feelings of anger, and mistakes, and even crises, etc.

B. You asked a broad question about the purpose of creating mortal man who is so deficient. As the Torah puts it, "For the inclination of man's heart is evil from his youth" (B'reshit 8:21). So why did G-d create us this way, with such strong physical inclinations?

The Torah is replete with metaphors of G-d because this is the only way we can understand; imagery and figures of speech from our own lives must be used. Every once in a while we have to stop and remind ourselves that these expressions are not to be taken literally. This is why I often say k'vayachol, which means "as it were" or "so-called."

But in truth, I believe that there is much more here than just an allegory or figure of speech. Our entire lives are a parable for something higher - and this is strongly indicated by the fact that we feel a constant drive for something more complete. What is this "more complete" something? It is our gradual ascent, in every realm; and there is no end to the number of steps, because absolute perfection is actually divinity.

For instance, we aspire to attain justice, order and direction in the world. We can certainly succeed in increasing justice in the world, but we are always quite aware that there is more to go –and this is precisely our aspiration for G-d, the source of complete justice. Or, consider the concept of beauty. We sometimes see such amazing beauty in the world, such as a perfect sunset over an open field, or over Jerusalem, or over the sea; or we take note of the rare beauty of a person – and we feel that we simply cannot contain it. We are overcome by the beauty as if we are kneeling under the weight of the splendor or of the yearning; or we feel such intensity that we cannot contain it. This means that we sense that there is a complete beauty that we are nearing but cannot totally reach. This "perfect beauty" is G-dliness. And so it is in other areas. That is, the allegory is uplifted, gradually becoming itself the "lesson" that we learn, and then the new lesson becomes the allegory for the next-higher lesson, and so on. Similarly, all the imagery in the Torah can be read either on a low, debased level, or with a more refined approach; it all depends upon the spiritual level of the reader.

Actually, this is also the beginning of the answer to your second question. When a person grows and expands his containing vessels (his abilities of understanding), but fills them not with light and suitable content, but with that which is low, coarse and evil – it is as if he is feeding an adult with baby portions; he will then resort to filling in what he needs in a crude and debased manner. Our test and challenge is always to aspire to that which is higher, that which is more appropriate for us, that which is stronger and more refined. When your level appears to you to be crude or low, it means you should rise up to a higher and more refined and abstract level.

If we had been created without physical urges, there would be no missions, aims and tasks in the world. If everything were already perfect, there would be no place at all for humans as creative and productive beings. This is explained at length by Ramchal[62] in his work Daat Tvunot, written as a discussion between the "soul" and the "intellect." If you would like to study it, for sure you'll be able to find a study partner in HaMakom...

Again, thank you for your comments.

–Meir

---

[62] he renowned scholar and Kabbalist Rabbi Moshe Chaim Luzzatto (1707-1746), of Italy, Amsterdam, and Acco

Jan. 21, 2013 12:59

Shalom Meir,

True, three months have passed, but as some would say, better late than never...

I connected very much to your description of the expansion and increase in precision and refinement. But it's still unclear to me why G-d is not depicted in the Torah as the model of perfection to which we would want to aspire. Why is He sometimes presented as angry, vengeful, and needy of admiration and sacrifices? Are these the good traits that the Torah recommends we adopt?

I hope I'll be able to come soon and we'll be able to continue talking; this topic might be a bit too heavy for email. By the way, what subject will you be speaking about this week?

Thanks and all the best,

Alon

Dear Alon,

Just this morning I thought about you, for some reason, for the first time since I wrote to you last time – and then suddenly today I see your email! I have no explanation for things like this, but they do happen every once in a while...

Regarding the subject that I will speak about this week, I formulated it like this:

"You're across the ocean, and I'm stuck here...

"You say that I fear love more than loneliness, that I'm afraid of being loved, afraid of the waves, of the sea, of the storms of life, of freedom, of the great spirit... You say that I'm the one running away, that you're calling me to come and be totally with you, and that even when we are close – an ocean separates between us..."

My plan is to study together Midrashim on Parashat B'shalach that deal with the Children of Israel standing at the Red Sea after having just left Egypt. These Midrashim discuss their fear of crossing the sea towards the great and exalted, as strange as this may sound.

As to your question, you're right that it is too weighty for email, and my offer to learn the Ramchal together still stands.

There is something good about almost every single trait and characteristic. G-d is angered because (among other things) we "need" Him to be angered. We need all sorts of imagery, including this one. We are like children who require boundaries, and sometimes even a sharp word spoken in anger – though the parent must not actually become emotionally angry, but rather put on a bit of a show (as explained in the Talmud and Rambam). A father who is apathetic to his son's antics sends a message of lack of caring. When a woman asks her husband, "Which necklace should I buy? Which one is nicer?" and he says, "Whatever you choose is fine with me," he is not politely giving her the freedom of choice. Rather, he is essentially telling her, "Your deliberations on this topic don't matter to me and I wish you would stop bothering me."

G-d, the Exalted and High, "descends" to the world to deal with our problems: the orphan's suffering, the widow's tribulations, the oppression of the downtrodden... Sometimes He does so with a smile, and sometimes with anger and strict judgement. Yes, G-d asks us for sacrificial offerings – not because He needs them, but because *we* need to know that He wants them. It is like when a child brings his mother a drawing or a flower, or anything very special to him, and what he needs is for her to say how much she wanted exactly that very thing. We are like G-d's children looking for our way to Him, we want a bond with Him like that between a son and a father. We want to gladden, to soothe, to give to Him. For His part, He of course needs nothing, but He wants to give us the sense that He wants and needs, so that we will feel close. And He, after all, created us with this mechanism; it is part of Creation. The human need to admire is the aspiration for the exalted and unattainable. This human need for a sense of security is part of Creation. We as mortals look for a leader, and we want to admire Him and feel that He needs us. It doesn't matter to us that He actually doesn't need us - nor can we even deal with the alternative; as humans, this is how we were created.

This way of thinking is very natural, to seek out a subject for your admiration – and the most important thing is to be yourself, be upright and true, and not to skip to a level you're not yet ready for. Humans need something to admire and strive for, and G-d has graciously given you this. With time, and as you become more refined, your admiration will be towards things that are more spiritual, such as good character traits, doing good for others, special wisdom, artistic talents, etc.

Much success always!

- Meir

CHAPTER 20

FORBIDDEN - THROUGH NO FAULT OF THEIR OWN

Aug. 12, 2012 10:22

Shalom Meir, how are you?

I'm going out with a very special girl, and I feel, finally, there might be a chance for a quality relationship that could perhaps lead to marriage. She admitted to me that she once, a few years ago, had relations with a non-Jew on a trip abroad. She was on a trip after the army, "young and foolish, with no responsibilities towards anything," as she put it. Like me, she is also coming closer to Judaism – and I am a Cohen, which I heard is a problem in this context. But since the subject is important and complex, and all in all I like her, I'll ask your opinion again: Are there any lenient opinions in Jewish Law for this situation?

Also, out of general interest, what is the law of a Cohen who suddenly finds out that his wife had been with a Gentile in the past?

Thanks,

Chaim

Aug. 12, 2012 10:22

Dear Chaim,

Your second question is generally an easier one since they're already married, and the laws are slightly different. Every case must be judged on its own merits, of course, but there are leniencies when the couple is already married.

Regarding the first question – sadly, there is no solution, other than in rare cases where certain extra factors can be checked. If you are actually considering a specific case, that is, you feel you have found your soul-mate, then certain things can be checked further, and then, given all the relevant factors, I could ask a top Halakhic authority about it. If such an authority would rule leniently, it would certainly be considered a major leniency, one that perhaps only a truly great authority could take upon himself in a very specific case. Therefore, you have to assume that apparently there is no other way, and that with all the pain – and believe me, it is great – you will have to separate.

Let's talk more by phone.

- Meir

Dear Meir,

Yes, of course my question concerns my specific case (otherwise I wouldn't be that interested in the topic). But despite my initial enthusiasm regarding this girl, and though there are very encouraging signs – finally! – I can't yet whole-heartedly say that she is my soul-mate and my true heart's choice.

I tried to explain this whole thing to her, and I saw that it was not at all easy for her. She said that in Judaism there is always room for repentance, and how could it be that there is no atonement for something that happened years ago.

This priesthood business is quite a story...

- Chaim

Chaim, Hi!

I now have a bit more time and peace of mind to write you what I wanted to write you a few weeks ago. I'm here in England to serve as a cantor, and they gave me a very nice rooftop flat, equipped with everything I need, overlooking the gray and green London horizon. Everything is very serene and peaceful – if I forget for a minute that I'm far away from the Holy Land.

The primary message of the Torah of Israel is, as is known, one of love, compassion, mercy, optimism, giving the benefit of the doubt, humility and respect towards each and every person, and seeing the good in everything. This is, after all, the explanation of the well-known response given by Hillel the Elder to the man who wanted to learn the entire Torah on one foot: "That which you hate, don't do to others. Now go learn the rest." That is, Hillel told him the general rule, and added that the remainder is a type of itemization. The problem is that sometimes, when you learn these details, you encounter some things that appear to negate the original principle, as well as all sorts of hard-to-understand prohibitions. For instance, you have finally found someone you might be able to marry, after so much searching and loneliness – and along comes the Halakhah and pries into your past and hers and disqualifies and separates. This is truly very hard. I fully understand both of you, and I just wish I had a way to alleviate the tremendous pain.

Of course, your grievance applies to life in general. A child is born with a defect; why must he suffer? Is he at fault? A person is hurt in a car crash, through no fault of his own; what did he do wrong? Or, as Amos Oz[63] writes in his book My Michael about a man who hears from his doctor that he has cancer and bursts out self-righteously: "How can that be?! I eat right, I do exercise, I pay my membership dues, I volunteer for reserve duty, I'm a model citizen! There must be some mistake!" But there is no mistake... Illegitimate children (mamzerim), as well, are born with a type of spiritual defect, through no fault of their own – but this does not have to hold them back from making great accomplishments in important things. The

---

[63] sraeli novelist and professor who died in Dec. 2018

Sages teach that a Torah scholar who is a mamzer takes precedence over an ignoramus Cohen. That is, one's personal achievements are many times more important than qualities with which one is born, such as ancestry.

Still and all, regardless of blame or fault, one's status in certain matters is determined at birth. Priests, as well, are born with a status of sanctity, whether they like it or not. It obligates them, and it restricts them significantly in terms of the women they may consider marrying. A divorced woman is not inherently flawed; on the contrary, one who is not a Cohen has a mitzvah to remarry his divorced wife if she has not yet become betrothed to another man. Still, she may not marry a Cohen. Similarly, a widow is not inherently flawed, and yet she is not permitted to marry a Cohen Gadol (High Priest). OK, that's only one or two in a generation, so it's not such a problem[64]. Certainly no one blames a married woman who was raped, for she was a victim who has suffered more than enough - but still, she may not marry a Cohen. The laws of the Torah are not a collection of rules of etiquette and niceties between people. Rather, if we believe in the Torah, this means that we necessarily believe that there is a system of ethics and logic that is greater than us, beyond our understanding; if we understood everything that G-d requires, the phrase

---

[64] Nowadays it doesn't apply at all.

"If I knew Him, I would be Him[65]" would apply.

Another example: The Torah calls a prostitute k'deshah, from the root meaning "sanctified" – and she is not forbidden to a Cohen. Who is forbidden to a Cohen? Only a woman who had relations with someone who is forbidden to her, even if only once. The Torah does not deal with fault, but only with the facts - permitted or forbidden, pure or impure - without assigning blame. And yet another example: It is clear to all that a woman's monthly cycle is a natural requirement for reproduction and the continued existence of the world, and still a woman in this state is called "niddah," meaning "ostracized." Furthermore, one is actually required to become impure by burying his close relatives who have died, yet it is a spiritual fact that the impurity of death is with him until he becomes pure.

However, beyond all of the above, the Torah charges the Sages of Israel to always look for the way that unites life and basic ethics, on the one hand, and the Torah and Halakhah, on the other. They are commanded to do as much as they can to find dispensations and Halakhic ways to permit a wife to her husband. It is incumbent upon them to connect and unite, to make life easier for people, and to distance them from rifts between nature and the Divine. This is why so many Halakhic responsa from all periods deal with such questions. The Sages of Israel

---

[65] Sefer Ha'Ikarim, end of 2,30

throughout history have made great efforts to find solutions. However – once they realize that their most strenuous efforts have not been successful, and that there is no Halakhic opening by which to rule leniently, the search to "solve" the situation is over. Rav Kook defined this situation so well in one of his works of responsa: "The Halakhic authorities are commanded to be compassionate, but where there is no Torah dispensation, we cannot be more merciful than G-d Himself."

Anyone who has seen Halakhic sages deliberating over a difficult question, and their crying and sorrow at not having found a solution, will find it easier to accept the situation. They will then know that arbitrariness and hard-heartedness have nothing to do with the Halakhic process. The journalist Shaul Maizlish, who wrote a book about former Chief Rabbi Ovadiah Yosef, told me that he remembers how Rav Ovadiah wept as he pored over Halakhic texts regarding the cases of young women whose soldier husbands were still missing after the battles of the Yom Kippur War, trying to find Halakhic ways to render them widows and no longer married – so that they could remarry and build new homes. Someone else told me that every day during that period, Rav Ovadiah sat and cried as he wrote Halakhic rulings. Incidentally, he permitted each one of the women whose cases came before him.

How can we explain these things in terms of G-d's

providence over the world and His providence over each person? Clearly, we cannot do so comprehensively – but to hear a voice, some kind of call or spiritual message, we certainly can. After Rabbe Nachman of Breslov's wife died, many different women were suggested to him as candidates for marriage, until he finally got married. He later said that actually each one of them was an eligible "marriage partner" in the world of souls. This was consistent with his approach that there are an infinite number of levels of "marriage partners," even amongst those who were merely suggested.

Perhaps this is a message of sorts for the Cohen, to reinforce and strengthen the significance of his being a Priest. Perhaps, too, this is a message for the woman, who must understand that her specific path to her husband must pass through an encounter with a Cohen, though it never had potential to begin with. That is, her path to establishing a family must be helped along by a greater spiritual uplifting and closeness to Hashem than would have happened otherwise.

Someone is taking care of you. And perhaps the meeting between you and this woman was designed so that each of you would help the other, at long last, find your respective intended spouses. These conclusions, of course, are ones that only the people themselves can come to, based on how their personal faith is strengthened by having undergone this crisis.

I pray from the depths of my heart, during these most special holy days, for the success of each of you in building true, devoted homes in Yisrael – homes full of love, sanctity, and continual Divine inspiration.

Chaim, if this letter helps you in any way, I would be happy if you would want to share it with her, or with anyone else whom it might be able to encourage. And if there is any further help I can give you in this matter, I would be glad to talk with either of both of you, or study the subject with you, or explain, or do anything else that could help.

May you have a good and sweet year, you and your family, present and future.

–Meir

Dear Meir, my friend,

Thank you so much for the detailed letter. I shared it with her and we talked about it. I think, just as you wrote, that it could very well be that the way in which we separated could enable us to help each other. Usually when people feel very close, it is easy for them to understand what type of person the other one needs, as long as they can rise above their "small" feelings. I think she, too, came away with this sense. I actually feared that this would estrange her from Judaism altogether, because she seemed quite upset the last time we met, but I was happy to see that this was not the case.

Many times, a crisis can help shape and develop us. Unfortunately, divorcees[66] and other "forbidden" women of different types are liable to develop various complexes and feel as if they are "second-rate" – while others who seek to understand in depth, and are lucky to find people from whom they can draw encouragement and wisdom during this "crisis," as you wrote, can actually grow from it.

You have given me strength to go forward, to deal with this story from a position of strength, and not weakness.

Good luck over there, and watch your health and your voice.

- Chaim

Dear Chaim,

My wife says that she imagines the world of souls up there as a collection of sacks filled with feathers. But there are many very different types of feathers. Sometimes we meet someone for whom we feel a particular affinity, as if "the two of us are from the same sack." It's a theme sometimes found in Hassidic stories, where the tzaddik has a dream that a certain person is a "soul-mate" of his, or will be his neighbor

---

[66] who may not marry Cohanim

in the World to Come. The tzaddik feels he must find out who this person is, and ends up being surprised that the other's way of life seems to be very different than his own - so he then begins the search for the secret, for the person's special good deeds or inner traits... Regarding our topic, just as we have a circle that includes only one's spouse, and a wider circle of family, there is also a circle of "souls from the same sack..."

See you soon,
Meir

CHAPTER 21

"YOU REALLY BELIEVE THERE'S LIFE UP THERE IN A WORLD-TO-COME?"

Dear Meir, Shalom!

My uncle, with whom I was very close, died last week in a car crash. He was relatively young, 62, and everyone loved him. Our family is broken and in shock. The whole family is totally not religious, but suddenly, during this week of the *shiva* mourning period, everyone is trying to act precisely according to religious law, asking a rabbi about every single thing. The strangest thing is that my uncle's daughter, who is the most anti-religious of all – she has no problem eating shrimp and the like – keeps asking about every detail of what she to do according to religion. This has led to discussions among us about the soul, and if it continues to exist somewhere, and the World to Come – all sorts of issues that we never brought up before.

My question is: Could you recommend a book of Jewish sources that analyzes in depth the topics of death and the World to Come, one that is appropriate for a secular family? We would like to read it in the framework of a family study session.

Thanks in advance,

Barak

Hi Barak,

There are instructive chapters regarding death in the book *Orot HaKodesh*, "Lights of Holiness," by Rav Kook; a bit difficult to understand, but with a very optimistic outlook. He explains there why the righteous do not fear death - and he in fact practiced what he preached, when he contracted cancer towards the end of his life. It's not really appropriate for reading during the *shiva* period, for it requires real concentration and clear thinking, but if I understood you correctly, you were referring to afterwards. It would be a good idea for you to prepare those chapter in advance and translate them into simpler language. If you need some help in preparing them, I would be happy to help.

In general, it's pretty hard to recommend a good book without knowing your family. There's another book called *Gesher HaChaim*, "Bridge of Life," which can be found in every store that sells religious Jewish texts. Its second part has special chapters on this topic, written in a clear style; flip through it and see if it's appropriate[67].

Meanwhile, I would just like to share with you some personal stories.

Sometime after my mother passed away, I saw her in a dream. We were sitting in a room and talking. At one point I ask her: "This whole World to Come

---

[67] At the time I wrote this, I wasn't aware of the excellent book compiled of Rabbi Joseph Soloveitchik's writings, "Out of the Whirlwind: Essays on Mourning, Suffering and the Human Condition."

thing – how much of it is real, definite, clear-cut? It's very hard for us to understand it." She answers: "I'll explain. The room that we're in now is dark, right? We can barely see the items in it. Now turn on the light. Look how clear everything is - concrete, sharp, with no doubts, right? That's exactly how the World to Come is for those in This World. You are all as if in a dark room, in which the items are very definitely present even though you can't see them clearly. But our existence here is most definitely concrete, and the fact that you can't see it is only because of your limited vision in This World."

The second story concerns my brother, who died at a young age. He was a genuine G-d-fearing Jew, and made sure even when he was sick to study Torah, to do kindness, to pray each of the three daily prayers – but what gave him the most pleasure was to put on tefillin. Every day, even under the most difficult of circumstances, even on his very last day on earth, he made sure to put on tefillin, even if it was only for one moment just before sunset. We had a few talks before his passing about Divine Reward and Punishment, about the different worlds, and about medical miracles. He suffered so much, and was a great believer. Several months after he died, he came to me in a dream. We began to debate, in the dream, which world was better – here in This World, or in his World to Come. Each of us made our case for our own world, and finally I told him, "OK, you say everything is great there, but explain to me how you are able to exist every single day without putting on tefillin; it must be torture for you!" He laughed and said, "You can't understand. Why are people in This World commanded to put on tefillin? It's because you're like slaves, running all day long from here to there, from this office to another, from the bank to the post office, one task after another – slaves. Inside the tefillin is a passage reminding us that we were slaves in Egypt and that G-d took us out so that we would be free. So once a day, when you put on tefillin, you receive a few moments of freedom and a reminder that true freedom is a human aspiration. But up here, we don't need that at all. Here, we're truly always free, there is no slavery at all, and so we don't need the mitzvah of tefillin."

And finally, a third story, told to us by Rav Avigdor Nebentzal, Rabbi of the Old City of Jerusalem when we were sitting *shiva*. He told of the Ramban[68] who had a very beloved student who was deathly sick. This was a tremendously difficult time for the Ramban, and he asked his student to promise him that when he reached the Upper World, he would find a way to appear to the Ramban and tell him how he was doing, and would also ask why he was taken from this world at such a young age. The student promised, and passed away. After some time, he came to the Ramban in a dream, and told him at length wondrous

---

[68] Nachmanides, 13th-century Torah giant of Western Europe and the Land of Israel

things about what he was experiencing in the World of Truth. The Ramban asked him, "And what of your promise to ask why you were taken at such a young age?" The student said, "Oh, that - I didn't ask. I can't explain to you why exactly, but when you come here, you see that it's just not a question."

I know these stories don't provide a philosophical explanation, and don't really touch on the issues of eternity. I just wanted to share these with you from my own personal vantage point. Perhaps something of these stories will touch you or one of your family members.

May all the mourners find comfort.

- Meir